BEGINNING AGAIN IN A FOREIGN LAND

Todos Santos and Pescadero, Baja California Sur, Mexico

Virginia Moonstone Mazzetti

Cover photographs by Laurie Bauer of Bay Laurel Photography
Author's portrait profile by Paty Raines

ISBN: 1545088721
ISBN 13: 9781545088722
Library of Congress Control Number: 2017905201
CreateSpace Independent Publishing Platform
North Charleston, South Carolina

TABLE OF CONTENT

This book is a collection of interviews with twenty courageous, single women who in the second half of their lives have relocated to the frontier state of Baja California Sur, Mexico. They have been many persons to many people, both at home and in careers, and now life seems to have opened up an opportunity for their energies to flow freely. They have had lifetimes of love and lessons and have met with courage the challenges of life so far, and yet they seek change. Change of place, culture, language, friendships, daily events, and habits.

They came for different reasons at different ages and have stayed. Why? Are these women energized by exercising the strengths they have developed over their lifetimes and looking forward to acquiring new strengths? Do they welcome new challenges? Do they feel that their old lives are over and that it's time to be reborn in a new place and time? Are they running from something, or are they walking curiously toward the unknown because it's fun?

Some of these women did not arrive yesterday but have lived, worked, written about, and traveled in Mexico for fifty years, twenty-six years, and seventeen years. One settled in a year ago after many adventures hiking and exploring the Baja. They have brought artistic talents and aspirations to further their art in a new, inspirational environment. Many have entrepreneurial spirits and want to try their luck and knowledge in a new context. One was drawn to and sucked in by the surfing beaches.

They all enjoy the easy weather and the stimulation of living in a different culture where different values shine a light on where they are from: California, New Mexico, New York, New Hampshire, Colorado, Texas, Kentucky, Washington state, Arkansas, Iowa, Canada, and England. They all share stories of their relationships and encounters with the Mexican people. Twelve of the twenty have bought land and built their homes. Others have rented houses more than once, renovated trailers, slept in tents for long periods, and house-sat as solutions to their housing needs.

They have all met the challenge of learning Spanish: using it to get what they want, reading it every day, speaking it on the phone, pantomiming, and listening in perplexity to the rapid-fire Spanish of Mexican locals. Forever and always they are learning lessons in patience. They've been taken advantage of and considered "the bank" by employees. They've been robbed and vandalized and lived through howling hurricanes, and yet they stay and say they love it here. Why? One reason is that they cannot afford to live a decent life in the United States of America. Their pensions, social security, investments, and so on are not going to pay the rent and buy food and run a car in the United States. Their money can stretch much further in Mexico. That alone can make a single girl happy!

Quite a few of these women came because spirit guided them to this place. There are lovely stories of faith and spiritual paths that guided them to overcome obstacles and doubts and that fortified their resolve to stay. Many advise readers to follow their hearts, their intuitions. Many experienced love at first sight for the towns of Todos Santos and Pescadero. That strong infatuation has been the glue in their resolve to stay the course.

Life got challenging when Hurricane Odile, a category 3-4 hurricane swept up the middle of the peninsula in September,

2014. All these brave women were here that night and the following weeks of reconstruction, debris removal, power outages and water shortage. Each contributor tells her story of those frightening hours endured alone and how they adjusted to the aftermath. We all witnessed the resilience of the Mexican people and their devotion to family and friends. I think the crisis made this place more our home rather than frightening us away.

Baja California Sur has always had strong ties with the United States of America, and the gringo population is quite entrenched in the small towns—to the benefit of the Mexican population, because gringos are, by comparison, phenomenally rich and generous. Many charitable programs have been started and maintained by the ex-pats, and the entire population has benefited. There is always a place to plug in efforts to give someone, young or old, a hand up. One of Baja Sur's strong points is that it is close to the States, so it is easy to visit family in the States or to get health issues checked in a US hospital. Another factor in the choice of places to live abroad is that we have the same alphabet. There's nothing like traveling halfway around the world and not being able to read the signs.

My hope is that the book will give some good, practical advice and encouragement to anyone, man or woman, who is thinking of moving home to Mexico. Baja Sur is a specific place, but Mexico is quite large and has many ecosystems and elevations to choose from. Check maps, and search the web. Mexico's history is so rich, and we didn't learn about it in our schools up north. Mexico is a fascinating study with many books about history and contemporary life. I have tried to find out why things are the way they are here and to get the Mexican side of the country's relationship with the United States of America.

I envision you reading a couple of interviews with your morning tea or coffee and imagining what it would be like to begin again in Mexico. I interviewed myself because no one else was available to interview that day. I put it as the first interview so that you would get to know the author a bit. It really doesn't say much about me, more about place. I love this place!

The air is fresh from the Pacific Ocean, until someone in the neighborhood burns plastic. Walking at sunset with my dog is a joy until I come across someone's trash dumped at the foot of a three-hundred-year-old cardon cactus. I live through puppy invasions that poke their way through the neighbor's fence, and I pick up their curios all around my property. It's not heaven all the time, and it feels like hell in the heat of August. But it is mostly quiet, pollution-free, and peopled by happy souls who love their families and eat a lot of tortillas and the freshest fish you can imagine. It's just one more slice of life, and I'm glad I have a piece of it to call home.

CHAPTER 1

MOONSTONE MAZZETTI

Arriving at Moonstone's gate, which is made of palm fronds battered by Hurricane Odile last September, made me think that I am about to enter a rancho in a *bosque* [forest]. I turned around once to see the landscape behind me: desert with sparse vegetation and blazing, hot sun. A sign said, "Ring the bell. *Toca la compana.*" I pulled the cord and waited for a response. The bell was melodious with several harmonious tones blended to perfection. Looking through the gate, I saw a little building with a porch covered with palm leaves (*palapa*) crowded with potted plants. There were thick trees behind the casita and to the right and left of it. Two barking dogs came to greet me, but don't look too ferocious for all their noise.

Here she came, the *dueña* [owner], with a broad-rim hat, sunglasses, and a long-sleeved white blouse covering her hands, a man's shirt for sure. Her skirt swished as she walked to the gate to unlatch it. She said, "Welcome. This is Lucy, the elder, and Cha Cha, the visitor. *Pasale [come in]*."

I knew Moonstone was a permaculture designer and had a small *vivero* [nursery], but I hadn't expected the look of verdant abundance that now surrounded me. Big trees, some flowering; lilies in bloom; palms of every description.

"Nice bell," I said.

"It's from India," she answered. "Some countries just have their metallurgy down."

"This little casa is the Tiny Tienda." She extended her arm to the *palapa*-covered porch. "It is my attempt to provide pure personal products to people who care what they wash their plates in, put on their bodies, brush their teeth with, and put in their soil. Actually, they are quality products that I miss from the United States and thought others might miss them, too."

I asked, "How's business?"

Moonstone said, "This time of year, all the nice oils and creams are in the house in the refrigerator because they can melt sitting on a shelf. So now the building is my art studio, where I paint, make hand-built pottery, and lay out patterns and fabric for sewing projects."

Moonstone and I walked to the house along a short, wide path I hadn't noticed because of the placement of the trees and plants. She had hidden her house from her public business very well. The porch where we arrive was cozy in size and decor. It was once again hidden from the road not thirty feet away by a sight barrier of areca palms and a gigantic, cardboard cycad bordering the stone patio. *Sweet*, I thought.

I asked, "Can you give me a tour of the house?"

She replied, "Sure. It doesn't take long. It's five hundred fifty square feet."

We entered the one great room with comfortable chairs, a desk, and bookcase at one end and on the other end, a tiny kitchen lacking gadgets and clutter on the small counters and a slim oak table and chairs.

She clarified her choices. "Now that I am not a mother of three or a northern woman filling up the root cellar every summer, I just wanted to be *out of* the kitchen and not spend a lot of time preparing meals. It is definitely not the selling point of the house. Most people would freak at its simplicity."

All the windows in the great room framed leafy bowers, which provided romantic, dappled, green light. From the kitchen, we entered the hall, housing the refrigerator and pantry shelves on the right and a bathroom on the left. The short hall led into the bedroom displaying a different botanical print on each of the three windows, a dust ruffle, and a bedspread.

"Biodiversity outside, biodiversity inside," stated the *dueña*. The closets were draped in fabric instead of doors, as were the bedroom and bathroom entrances. She stated, "What I noticed about the concrete houses here is how much they echo, so I wanted to use lots of fabric instead of harder surfaces, like wood. And as my friend says, 'Doors are overrated.' That, and I love the weaving arts. Mexico has world-class weavers."

Author- Do you own or rent?

Moonstone (MS). I own the property and designed the house for my needs and pocketbook. It was built eight years ago, and this is my seventh year of living year-round.

Author- I didn't know there were seasons here.

MS. I thought that too, until I lived here awhile and saw what the plants do and how the wind blows stronger in the winter than in the summer. A lot of endemic trees lose their leaves in the spring here, unlike where I came from in north-central Washington. That really threw me, and I worried that trees were dying. But, no, they grew new leaves really quickly. Before I built my house, I had never spent a summer here. The heat and directness of the sun straight overhead are a force to consider in the design of the house and landscape.

Moonstone was referring to the fact that Todos Santos is situated directly on the Tropic of Cancer, which means that it is the furthest north the sun ever travels. That puts the sun directly overhead on the summer solstice and the months preceding and following the solstice.

Moonstone continued, "Also the true tropical plants and trees love the heat and are magnificent in the summer, but they can look brown in the leaf in the winter months if it gets too cold. And it does get cold here. This is still North America, don't ya know?"

Author- How did you come to this part of Mexico to live?

MS. My son who surfs started to build a house up the coast from Todos Santos just two miles. He worked on it only in the winters with whatever money he had for the project. It took him and his girlfriend and buddies who came down to learn how to surf eight years to totally finish it. He invited me to come down because, "Mom, we're going to be there for months. Come and stay awhile."

I had been having trouble with cold-induced asthma in the northern winters and wanted to get out of the wood-heated, smoky cabin and into the sun. So, I came and had a blast with all the young people and the one other mom who came down. I kept the garden up and made the compost pile and huge salads for dinner. I took a lot of walks out of the construction noise to paint in watercolors and practice a movement therapy I was into then. I came for eight winters and fell in love with Todos Santos and the area. I always thought snow was so alien. I love the climate of fewer clothes and the delightful night temperatures most of the year.

Author- Does your son still live here?

MS. No. As all young people do, he followed his career and opportunities. He lives back in the States now. Their place is now a rental. He gave me fair warning that that was coming. I had to decide if I wanted to buy an RV and camp on the beach, house-sit, travel around Mexico, or buy land and build a house, as I had witnessed so many others doing. I would never have done the latter except for the eight years of watching my son deal with a contractor and Mexican workers.

I looked for land within walking distance of his house and bought half an acre, or two thousand square meters. The Mexican owner, as they are want to do, bulldozed the property to remove a burden of trash and everything else except a very old, huge cardon cactus and one other cardon. Nothing. It was a fill-in-the-blank situation. I loved it because I had, in the past, with the help of family and friends, brought four other sites from nothing to productive, organic-farming and hobbit-type living spaces.

I was a back-to-the- land hippie for thirty-two years before I settled in here. I have studied permaculture (PC) and have a PC design certificate and have laid a hundred miles of drip irrigation in a dry climate. North-central Washington is in the rain shadow of the Cascade Mountains and has an average rainfall of six inches per year I started planting the periphery with trees and waited for the title to come before I built the house. There was plenty of time to design the house on paper and with rocks and sticks on the ground.

Author- You didn't have an architect help you with the design?

MS. No, because I knew I wanted small. I don't like housework. I am a fan of a fascinating book called *A Pattern Language* by six international architects. It was commissioned by the mental-health board of California. The authors observed what worked for people in different cultures around the world, what in their environment made them happy. I had read the book twice before I ever got to use it to design a house. I was thrilled! Part of the thrill of designing the whole lot and then pulling it off was that there was no man to tell me I couldn't do something and no hippie-commune council to consult with. The opportunity came at the best time of my life. I was sixty-one and had decades of experience caring for plants with drip irrigation. And money! The dream was propped up by an inheritance, which I managed like the true hippie non-consumer that I am. I actually made a site plan as I was shown in the permaculture design class and stuck to it.

Author- You must like Todos Santos and lower Baja to have stayed. Why?

MS. In my mid-twenties, I lived in Jackson Hole, Wyoming, and saw the benefits of living in a tourist town. Tourists are usually happy people. When money is changing pockets, the locals are happy, so the vibe is high. Also, tourist towns tend to dream up things for tourists to do. So here we have a music festival, art festival, historic-house tour, Hispanic film festival, GastroVino festival, and wonderful restaurants with live music any time of day or night. It has a yin-yang social life; the snowbirds return in the winter months, and the social life is almost too much. Then in the summer when there are fewer people, life can be really slow and undemanding. Mostly I like the climate.

Author- Have you had many challenges here

MS. About a thousand! [*She rolled her eyes and agitated in her chair, her hands grasping each other.*] Which one do you want to hear about first? How about finding a gardener to help? The older, married guys are steady and show up, but they don't like to be told what to do, especially by a woman. They do what they know, which is not permaculture compliant. The younger ones are a no-show because their buddy whisked them away to the beach that day. I had one *muchacho* [young man] who liked to learn about permaculture, and he loved plants. That was fun and a blessing for seven years—when he bothered to come. But then he ended up in rehab, and I haven't seen him since.

Another challenge is living with geckos and their poop and their surprising appearances when you least expect them. How about cockroaches? Every year there is one insect that dominates. It never seems to be the same here. One year it was cockroaches in the house. One year there was a white-fly epidemic throughout the entire region. Last year there was a black-butterfly migration that lasted two months, and you had to do a windmill arm dance to discourage their entry before opening the door. If you didn't help them back out, their bodies would be gone in the morning—only the wings left, eaten by geckos.

And let's not forget the dust. After the main road a block from the house got paved, the dust problem abated, but I think it was a cause of some of my lung problems. When I left Washington, I knew there would be challenges, but at least they would be new ones. I needed a change of everything. I was in a rut. My kids had left home. The husband had created a business west of the mountains and was never home. I couldn't get excited for one more canner pot of tomatoes for the root cellar. I kept asking myself, "What's on the other side of the hill?"

Author- Is life different for you here?

MS. In some ways, it's the same, because I still like to spend time at home. That's why I have a home-based business called Wholesome Home and Garden. [*Her blog is at http:/pcfsbaja.blogspot. mx/.*] Just like when I lived in the mountains up north, I go to town once a week. When I get there, I'm amazed that I live in Mexico. The lifestyle I chose decades ago is still my motice operenti: to live close to the earth, simply and quietly, and to be a world citizen caring for the earth wherever I live. I'm not looking to join another culture and adopt a lot of restrictive boxes.

One thing that is different is the number of keys I keep track of: four for the house, three for the Tiny Tienda, three for my son's house, and three for the rental casita. I never had keys before. I had to get used to locking all the windows and doors before leaving the house. My house has been entered and stolen from five times because I was too casual and naïve.

Author- Have you integrated into the Mexican culture?

MS. Not really. I have few Mexican friends, and that is one reason why my Spanish skills never increase. I don't listen to it enough or speak it. I start to speak, and English comes out. I've taken three long class series where I reach a plateau and can't absorb anymore. Todos Santos is a bilingual town, and I'm good at pantomiming what I need. But that doesn't help me in a doctor's office. I think I'm missing out, but I'm shy and back away from difficult situations. I do speak Spanish with my worker and helpers, but it's a sort of Spanglish.

I have an affinity with the Mexicans, because I lived and worked for three decades in organic agriculture and strove to be self-sufficient on our homestead. My entire family worked seasonal jobs together. We lived on a subsistence income and knew the importance of community.

Author- Are there things about the Mexican culture you like and dislike?

MS. I like mañana, though it reinforces my procrastination habit. In harsher climates, there is always a push to get something done. Here you are guaranteed that another beautiful day will follow, so you can do it later. I like siesta, because it is healthy and it's a tradition. Unlike the driven lifestyle in the States, it is acceptable to take time out to relax during the daylight hours.

I like how they put family first, no matter what other pressures are put on them. They seem to be happy people who enjoy themselves when they're together. My neighbors have a party, and there is no music and constant laughter. If there is one Mexican, there are bound to be two or three. If there are three Mexicans, then there are six. If there are six, there are twelve, and there's a party going on. It's a very social culture, but most rural, land-based cultures the world over are more social than intellectual. I have learned to drink water from my Mexican workers: a whole bottle at once. No sipping for me anymore. Stay hydrated!

Author- What was Hurricane Odile like for you and all these beautiful plants?

MS. It was frightening and a lot of work cleaning up. It was so loud, like a freight train passing by your house for seven hours. I got to witness which trees were flexible and which ones were rigid and lost limbs. Every leaf was gone. Whole bushes were gone.

One and a half fence lines went down, and the electric-meter pole was in the mud. I was without electricity for two and a half weeks. Temperatures were in the nineties and hundreds for the whole month of cleanup, with no fans or ice. Some days I was in a panic to get to town and sit in front of a fan.

Because some roads in northern Baja got damaged and no trucks were running, I watched the shelves in the stores go bare. Beer and Coke were the first things to sell out. There was no drinking water or ice in town for two weeks until electricity got restored. I was fortunate to have two workers who came every day. The *palapa* roof on the carport blew off. It didn't go far and wasn't damaged. I watched Manuel put it back on four new posts all by himself, inch by inch, propping and moving it slowly into place. Mexicans work hard in great heat.

The town itself suffered serious tree loss. A week after the event, I watched two senoritas walk hand in hand, smiling, down a totally wrecked street. They are a resilient bunch. I must also give tribute to the Mexican electric company, CFE, for their quick and thorough response to the emergency here and in Cabo San Lucas and San Jose del Cabo. We found out that the Mexican Army is rated number one in the world for responding to emergencies. Odile came after four months of extreme heat, which continued during a month of cleanup. I was exhausted and headed for Berkeley, California, for R and R. When I crashed on my friend's guest bed, I didn't wake up for nineteen hours.

Author- How's your love life?

MS. Up until this past year, I had none, not even a date. I am happy being alone, but you start to wonder after a while. I started a singles group, hoping to at least have some men friends. I'm not interested in having a boyfriend or husband. Twenty-eight years of being the heart and servant of the family was enough for one lifetime. It is nice to hear what men have to say after only having women friends. Plus I always get in nuts-and-bolts, how-do-you-do-it questions. Right now I am enjoying the attention of a gringo who is talkative and helpful and likes to go out to eat, but I have to keep saying that I don't really want to be somebody's something, like a girlfriend. I have risen to the occasion of facing the world alone after such a long marriage. I'm stronger and more confident than I was. And more skillful.

Author- What are your plans for the future?

MS. I am turning my first propagation shed into a rental casita. I'm going to rent it out to friends of friends and try to make some money, since my inheritance just now ran dry. I hope it works, because my previous life did not include too many employers who could afford to pay social security: organic farmers, orchardists, and a Japanese camp where I planted a full garden to eat when the campers came in July. In rural places, people often work under the table and then get no credit for what they earned.

My body is constantly being tested during the hot season, which is mid-July through October. Right now I have sun poisoning from too many years of unprotected exposure to the sun. My love of outdoor living and working is not compatible with my aging skin. I have started to wonder about other places to live, but where? I don't want to return to the United States, and I finally have the right to be a permanent resident of Mexico.

Moonstone was referring to a law that had changed. In the past, she showed up at the emigration office every year and paid to renew her resident status, thereby earning permanent resident status in nine years. Now emigrants seeking that status have to prove they have a monthly income of US$3,000. It seems that every two years, a law changes that affects emigrants.

Moonstone continued, "The central mountains of mainland Mexico are said to be a lovely climate year-round, but it takes scouting and time and money to go find a place. I'm content here and love my place, so I will live another hurricane, hot season here and see if it agrees with my ever-changing, aging body."

Author- Does your family come down to visit?

MS. Yes. Usually all of them come in the winter and stay at my son's house. Even the ex comes with his latest girlfriend. My granddaughter has come once. We have fun, and they overbuy at Costco so that when they leave, I inherit a lot of good food, which is much appreciated. My second son, Johnny, who brought my stuff down eight years ago in his truck and cargo trailer and then stayed to help me finish the house, rents a room or house in La Ventana on the Sea of Cortez to play at windsurfing. That is fun. I get to go visit him.

Author- Any regrets?

MS. Not one. I was scared to live in Mexico by myself at first, but it was all in my head. Nothing scary has ever happened. Well, no. One night a young gringo living in a hovel up the street got robbed at gunpoint. [*Unusual for here.*] That was too close to home. I decided that since I didn't want to live in fear, I should just take precautions and lock the doors at night. I am really happy in my choice, and I totally enjoyed turning this half acre of desert into an oasis of endemic and exotic trees. The plants are so wonderful to watch grow and are so contented to be themselves. They are a wonderful example to me. Bloom where you are planted, and don't wish you could be something different than who you are. Glory be!

CHAPTER 2

BARBARA CHICK

I became friends with Barbara when she first came to Baja Sur twelve years ago. She and another woman, Christina, and I had all been recipients of inheritance—similar amounts even—and we were all single and the same age, mid-fifties. We marveled at that coincidence and bonded immediately. We had lots of stories to share back and forth about children, guilt, dreams for the money, and starting a new life in Baja. We are all still friends and live close to one another.

As I have witnessed Barbara's life here—her struggles with housing, health, family, and money—the word "intrepid" came to mind. While interviewing her, the word flashed in neon in my brain so much that I had to get the dictionary to check the meaning: "Intrepid: resolute fearlessness, fortitude, and endurance." Spot-on. Does this sound like the creed of an adventurer?

With her hands stretched wide and her eyes swelling to twice their resting size, she practically flew across the table and said, "*I love adventure*! I married my first husband after knowing him for only six days because he was going around the world and asked me to come. We went around the world twice and then got divorced. My second husband was a true adventurer, and with him, I had four children and lived in wilderness and poverty. The third husband was my true love, and his death broke my heart and took me down to reckless driving. I'm glad I'm still alive. For all the challenges, I am happier now than ever in my life. I've found peace and have escaped the system of the United States. I never fit into the American culture and will never live there again."

Barbara was from Santa Cruz, California, before her whole family moved to Salida, Colorado. With the passing of her mother came the money to flee the north country and find a place of solace where she could process the deaths of her mother, father, and third husband, which all occurred within five years. She drove a motor home down the peninsula by herself with the companionship of two dogs and a cat.

She told me, "The motor home broke down seventeen times from Colorado to Baja Sur! It stopped running every one hundred feet of travel in the Joshua Tree National Monument. The park rangers hated me and finally just towed me off to a side road. I held up traffic for hours at the border crossing. I was stuck three days in a driveway in San Pedro."

Moonstone (MS). Did you know Spanish?

Barbara Chick (BC). Not a word.

MS. Were you scared or frightened by the experience?

BC. Not really. I just prayed all the time. Your readers should know I have the faith of a born-again, spirit-filled Christian since 1971. Jesus is my savior; God is my heavenly father, and the Holy Spirit is my power and comforter. I see my life like this all the time...every day.

Barbara's destination was the beachfront property her brother had bought two miles south of Pescadero.

BC. I wanted to reckon with death. I parked the motor home and built a small *palapa* for shade on the dunes and talked to God, the water, the beach, and the marine life. There was no one on the beach. I planted bougainvillea and transplanted wild things and

13

collected and strung shells. I developed a water system of *tenacos* [storage tanks] and bought water delivered to the site in trucks.

Moonstone and Christina came out to visit and encourage me in my simplicity. We got to know each other. I didn't have a car. I was there for six months until my visitor's visa ran out. I didn't want to go back to the States, so my friends suggested I get a FM3 [*a* rentista *status, which doesn't exist anymore*]. Moonstone invited me and my dogs and cat to move onto her son's property two miles from Todos Santos. I had a car by then. I did a couple of moves after that, property sitting when gringos returned to the States. My daughter decided to join me, and I was delighted to have her.

Soon I bought a one-third acre in the slump of a hill in Las Brisas, a *colonia* [neighborhood] of Todos Santos, and designed a small house based on one I'd been in. The big plan was to have an end-of-life care center with five adjoining casitas. Mexican law put a damper on that dream, but I still enjoy the idea of it happening.

MS. That must have been a total experience: creating your own home in a foreign land. Challenging?

BC. I'd say. I designed it and hired a gringo contractor who wasn't a contractor. I learned that some contractors just do what they want to do-- *maybe all he knew how to do*-- instead of what you want them to do. It became stressful, and a Venezuelan girlfriend moved onto the property to help me relate to the workers in Spanish. She turned into a tyrant and wanted more money for her services, and one time she even asked me to leave. About that same time, I suffered nerve damage from an inept dental technician giving me Novocain, and it developed into trigeminal neuralgia, with a suicidal pain level of ten, which was unbearable and debilitating.

I moved back to the beach motor home to avoid stress and actually gave up my power to the Venezuelan. I endured that jaw pain for six years. At times I couldn't eat, swallow, or drink warm or cold beverages. I couldn't even talk. Also, I was living on two hundred eighty dollars a month.

MS. I remember that time really well, Barbara. You used to carry around a Spanish hand fan to put in front of your face when you grimaced in pain. We would be talking, and you would say, "I have to go now; the pain is coming on." Every time you came over, I fed you. I admired you for the diet you developed—blends of herbs that you grew, and eggnog from your own chickens every day for protein. I loved treating you to lunch in Pescadero. You got really skinny at one point. I was really happy for you when your sister found the doctor in the United States who developed the surgery to find that hidden nerve and cauterize it.

BC. I also made a Crock-Pot of beans and rice. Living like a real Mexican. I remember once you gave me a one-thousand-peso bill that your son had just given you.

MS. On his way out the door, he handed me this money, and I hadn't become attached to it. I hadn't already spent it on the wish list in my mind. You needed it, and the lift it gave you...a smile for your day, my dear.

[*Money is a weird phenomenon. It's supposed to change hands and go from pocket to pocket. But people worry about the next buck, so they hold on for security's sake. I love that memory, too, as well as the thought of my generous son and all the times he has helped me move and settle in places and then passed me a buck or two.*]

MS. You like it here, but it sounds like you have overcome some grand hurdles and risen to meet some demanding challenges.

BC. I love the Mexican people and some of their ways. I recently joined the Catholic church. I have always gone to church, and I have explored a lot of venues in Baja. I feel like I reached the heart of Mexico within the Catholic church. Mexicans put family first and will always stop and talk for a while. They teach us gringos not to push the river. Mañana is soon enough.

MS. Has your Spanish improved over the years? Did you ever take a class?

BC. Never took a class, but I keep speaking. And I am courageous about speaking out and being laughed at. Actually, that is what I do to open up friendly relationships…let them have a laugh on me.

Barbara is so expressive with her hands. Tall with dark, soft, wavy hair, she looks you right in the eye when she is talking to you.

MS. I know your history here, but there is one part missing: living in Pescadero. How did that come about?

BC. I was in my home in Las Brisas only a short while when my daughter married a Canadian and became pregnant with their first child. His house really had no walls, only slats and screen. Even the roof was like that. My daughter sought more security for her young son, so I just had to offer her my house. I built a small casita in the corner of the lot and tried living there, but it wasn't good…no *amable* [loveable, kind, nice, helpful, friendly].

So, I took the last of the inheritance and built a six-thousand-dollar, two-story *palapa* in a *huerta* [irrigated land] down the highway in Pescadero. There they grew peppers and basil and more. I was surrounded by Mexicans and crops and a clean sweep of a view to the ocean with no houses. Water galore. I planted to my heart's content until it was a jungle. It was sort of the gringo dream of living in a warm climate: living outside, kitchen and bathroom outside. The upper deck was my bedroom, open on three sides. There was a small RV parked under that deck, but I never really lived in it—just when I was contracted in a fetal position from the pain in my jaw.

MS. Sounds kind of nice and kind of rugged. I visited you there a lot and loved the vines and flowers. Your love of all that life was infectious. Were there challenges to that life?

BC. Oh, yes! There really was no house, so I was always contending with bugs…cockroaches, flies, mosquitoes, and *bobos* [gnats].

Geckos would fall on me from the *palapa* roof while I slept, and a chicken would climb the steps and sit on my stomach in the morning. [*She grimaced at the memory.*] Plus, my next-door neighbor would siphon gas out of my car, and my laptop went missing. I didn't want to go back after Odile took it down."

MS. You never complained about that place! You seemed to abide in such gracious contentment there.

BC. Well, I did a lot of Bible study and was a member of the Jehovah Witness group then. They helped me out. Also, my son-in-law built steps, making the bathroom and kitchen less rustic. There were two grandsons by then, and I felt good that they were in my house and my daughter felt more secure.

MS. So now you are in Todos Santos. How did that come about?

BC. Remember my telling you that if a big wind happened, the *palapa* would come down, because I had seen rot and termite damage in the posts? It had been standing for about seven years, which is about the life of a post in the ground here. Well, that's what happened.

Barbara was shifting in the chair, and she was gripping the sides with her strong hands. Her face had turned serious, with shadows of worry lines in the forehead.

BC. That's exactly what happened. The two *palapa* roofs came down, one on top of the other. There they sit to this day. I am basically homeless. I have been house-sitting ever since. I'm in the fourth one now. It is exhausting, moving around with possessions in tow.

[*Odile drove everyone's life and style to a new reality. Cleaning up, standing things back up, and hauling away the downfall was a mind-bending, wallet-wrenching experience. When the gringos returned to their properties in October and November, they were shocked and reassessed their holdings here. How much do you invest in something that is going to blow down? Landscapes were totally changed. People had clearer views of the ocean and their neighbor's bedroom window, which they had never seen before. To this day, 9 months after the hurricane, people still step over downfall, because the cost and effort of removable seem insurmountable. After an economically depressed summer (which is always the case in this tourist town), money was flowing into the workers' pockets by doing cleanup. I was truly happy for them to get the boon of work and the easing of income tension.]*

MS. So what are your options now for living here?

BC. I am rebuilding in the corner of my daughter's lot. The little casita I had built there long ago blew down, so now I have to rebuild on a no-budget scale. [*Another slice of life for Que Barbara! This girl has pluck!*] Money seems to always be a challenge. But God is a good provider, and living on the edge builds faith. I love my life here. You can't be poor and thrive in the United States. Maybe the mañana effect stretches time to include ease, and it is a marvel how things materialize effortlessly sometimes. I love projects! I roll things along, and then they come alive with momentum.

MS. How do you spend your time, what do you do (besides adjust to adverse circumstances)?

BC. My days are full. I love and devote time to people, dogs, and plants. I pray and praise God, because I am so grateful to be alive in such a beautiful place. I am never, never bored. I don't know if I have ever been bored! [*I was talking to an engaged human, here, curious and interested in the life and people around her.*] The book *The Power of Now* really hit me hard. I never read very much of it. The title alone launched me into an appreciation for staying in the present. And what do I have now?

Barbara's hands were flat on the table, like she was going to spring forward to hear my answer.

MS. Two dogs, three cars—

BC. I have Moonstone!

Barbara was right. Here we were at my table, totally enjoying this review of her life and our association over the years. She was an excellent example of being in the present.

MS. What things don't work for you here?

BC. I find it frustrating getting things I want from the States. It is all such a manipulation of time and people traveling and trusting the postal service. Patience is a virtue.

Barbara and I ended on a happy memory moment; we relived walking around the ejido where I had eventually bought the half acre (two thousand square meters) of desert where I made a home. Ejidos are sections of land that the Mexican government allots to their citizens so that every Mexican can have a piece of land. It was part of the land reform that was fought for in their civil war of the early twentieth century. There is a lot to say about the ejido system. But I am no expert, so enough said.

At that time Christina and Barbara had been helping me to decide what to do and where to buy. Dry country; no trees. I believe it was overgrazed at one time. There was a corner lot sharing a back corner that touched Christina's lot. I liked that the two roads would keep the next settlers at a distance and that there was a view of the ocean in a V-shaped depression caused by an arroyo, which ran on the other side of the road in front of the lot. I bought it, and before it was even fenced, Barbara suggested that we camp out on it to claim it as mine, to be a presence and feel it out. My son had the perfect tent. We pitched it in a front corner and had a good fire and sleep-out. I have pictures of the next morning. What happy smiles! We were all living our dreams—or starting to.

CHAPTER 3

JANICE BAILEY

I met Janice Bailey eight years ago when I was asked to help her check and correct the index of a book she was writing on magnetic healing. The book had been reformatted, so all the page references were wrong. It was winter, close to Christmas, and while Christina and I checked pages and learned the content of this incredible book, Janice would sit down at one of the two baby grand pianos in her living room and play Christmas carols. Or she would put on a CD of Christmas music and sing along. She even decorated her house with symbols and colors of the season.

I eyed Christina and whispered, "I bet we could talk her into having a caroling party."

This was sort of under-the-table talk, since gringos in Baja want to avoid the old pressured version of Christmas we had all lived for so many years. But I love Christmas with all its musical tradition, special food, and decorations. We proposed it to Janice, and she agreed to do it. For seven years, she led a choir of Mexican *niñas*, kindergarten through sixth grade, singing sacred music. She invited her old choir to come, and Christina and I invited everyone we thought might enjoy a sing-along.

At first, we sang from sheet music while Janice directed us. When the senoritas left, the rest of us retired to Janice's big, outdoor living room and sang every Christmas song we knew, sacred and popular, as we rocked on the swinging chairs, clapped our hands, and laughed with the songs as we remembered them. Not your northern Christmas, it was a warm evening on the porch. We harmonized, we disharmonized, we hooted, and we sang some twice to get them right. It was one of my favorite Christmases in Baja. I love when friends sing together.

Janice lives in a straw bale house she built in 2000. The living room has a cathedral-height, *palapa* ceiling with white walls, white floor, and white cushions on the furniture; two big, blue wall hangings; and intriguing wooden artifacts in windows sills and wall niches. She was the first to build with straw bales in the area, and she didn't know how—neither did the workers. No contractor would take her on.

At that time there was no hardware store in Todos Santos, so all supplies had to be brought from La Paz or Los Cabos, forty miles away on a two-lane, no-shoulder, death-trap highway. The old road had no culverts or bridges, so if there was a hurricane all the *vados* [dips] were flooded, and you couldn't go in either direction. If it was raining, you had to get your shopping done by one or two o'clock, before the vados filled with water.

Janice went knocking on doors in the town of Constitution and asked where she could buy straw bales; the existence of straw bales meant that there had to be a baler in working order. During the building process, a young man from Durango happened by. He knew how to use a chainsaw and used to cut huge pine trees for telephone poles. She bought him a big chainsaw from the loggers in Oregon so that he could make beams and shelves out of eucalyptus blowdowns from the last hurricane.

The house's bathroom has a Japanese sitting tub. The kitchen cabinet doors are painted in a mural by a local Mexican artist. She divided her big bedroom upstairs into two bedrooms to share with her mother and father when they came to visit. She knew how to move a big project forward.

We were sitting in her neat and tidy office on the second floor. She wanted the interview here so she could access her photo and memorabilia albums. I asked her "When and why did you first come to the Baja peninsula?"

Janice Bailey (JB). In 1985, while doing dishes in Texas, I heard a big voice with the force of a locomotive say, "Go to Baja!" I didn't know anybody in Baja, but I went to a seminar in San Diego soon afterward, rented a car, and drove across the border. I got as far as Ensenada and was not impressed. I gave a fisherman who asked me for water a ride, and he mentioned Todos Santos, "a sweet little town down by the tip." I had three more days, so I flew down to Cabo and took the bus up to Todos Santos. As soon as I got off the bus, I fell in love. It was quaint and clean, with water running down the street. The air was beautiful. I went back to Texas. But my kids didn't want to come, so I had to wait about ten years to resettle here, around 1996. I returned for short periods to visit. I knew I wanted to live here, but I had to finish up things in Texas. When I returned to stay, I lived with a Mexican family until I had a plan.

MS. Did you speak Spanish then?

JB. Yes. I have a BA and master's in Spanish and taught Spanish at all levels: kindergarten through college. As a teenager, my father worked in the embassy in Chile, so the whole family lived in Chile. In college, I returned to Chile on a summer break, which is their winter, to learn to ski. Eventually I became a Mormon missionary and stayed for two years, improving my Spanish and doing music for the church. We had a soprano, tenor, piano, and me on violin. We toured up and down the length of Chile playing classical music. I taught Chilean people how to read music, and we formed choirs.

It was quite the experience. It's a beautiful country settled by lots of Europeans, Italians, Germans, Nazis. Earlier the conquistadors had killed off most of the Indians or they had fled to the south, so it was very European. There are occasional towns and rivers with Indian names, but basically the indigenous people were wiped out. I had to learn Spanish at that time. When I returned, I was able to go quickly through college Spanish classes and got a BA in Spanish. I went to many colleges in Virginia, Utah, and South Carolina, and when I got married, we moved back to Virginia. I got a scholarship in Spanish through the National Defense Education Act. Eventually I got my master's in Spanish and Latin American history from Texas Christian University. My thesis was published by the Mexican government. It was an honor.

MS. I'm impressed! What was it on?

JB. It was about the Mexican historian Alfonso de Teja Zabre. He was *the* national historian and wrote a lot of books that I had to read and translate. He was very cultured and wrote in French also. There were books of poetry, too. I had my first daughter then. When I got pregnant with the second one, I didn't want to just sit around, so I decided to write another book. I entered a history-writing contest. I had heard of a man, Diego Ortiz Parilla, born in 1714, who mapped the Baja and then was sent to map and defend a certain mission in what is now Texas.

I went to Sevilla, Spain, and got permission to use the archival library, which had all the diaries, writings, and reports of the viceroys, conquistadors, missionaries, and so on of New Spain. I had to translate all these handwritten documents in archaic Spanish about horses, cannons, Indians, forts. I found a diary by a soldier who went on this journey; he was sent to map, explore, and fight Indians up to the Red River. It had never been translated. That was a challenge I enjoyed. I even went to a mansion in Mexico City to photograph a huge, life-size painting of an Indian uprising at the mission that Diego Ortiz Parilla was in charge of where two friars were killed. I won first prize in the contest, winning one thousand two hundred dollars, which back then was a lot of money.

By the time I had my third child, we had moved to New York state. I did homeschooling so we could travel. My husband was a pilot, so we could fly for a reduced rate. I focused the learning on music. I had heard of a Japanese man, Shinichi Susuki, whose family had a violin factory that made child-size violins after seeing all the orphans after World War II and wanting to help them. He figured out a way to teach three-year-olds how to play the violin.

I wanted to learn this method, so we went to Japan and studied. My firstborn was only three. She eventually played for the empress of Japan. My second daughter learned violin when she was three. By ages five and seven, they could play Bach and Vivaldi. I formed us into a trio, arranging the music and making costumes, even tuxedos. We were called the Fiddlers Three. We even worked out some choreography and had three shows at performance level. We did it for seven years. We played at the Winter Olympics in Lake Placid, New York, in Peru, in Acapulco, and in the big bull ring in Mexico City on Children's Day.

Janice got out a scrapbook, and I saw some incredible pictures of the three of them. It is always a treat to see photos of my friends as they looked when they were younger. So beautiful! Her children to this day have kept up the family tradition of music as art. Leslie, Janice's firstborn, has seen her daughter graduate from Berklee in Boston, playing the harp. One winter Leslie and all her children lived at Janice's while they migrated from Australia to the United States of America.

They put on the most beautiful concert in the church here in Todos Santos, playing harp, violin, cello, and piano and singing with trained voices. Dressed in white, they carried long, white candles in a procession down the central aisle of the church to take up their positions on the stage and made the most beautiful music ever to be heard in our church, which was all decorated for Christmas. The fact that it was a family of three generations of skillful musicians, all female, was so exquisite. The whole evening was an evening of pure beauty. I will always remember it.

JB. Here I have found various pianist who wanted to play together. But mostly they are in La Paz, so it is not so easy to get together. I played with a Mexicana named Quichu who helped to start the piano museum in El Triunfo. She is responsible for collecting many of those pianos. I played and worked with Luis Pelaez from La Paz, who played the violin. Quichu, Luis, and I formed a trio and enjoyed our time playing together. He wanted to start a symphony orchestra here. I helped him with that project. I got to see him conduct the orchestra the other night in the plaza in a ten-year-anniversary celebration of Todos Santos becoming a Pueblo Magico. It felt good to see a dream come true.

MS. So when did you buy this land and start to build the house?

JB. I came back by myself in 1995 to 1996, ready to make home. I bought this property which is two thousand square meters, or half an acre. It was a blank piece of earth. There were none of these palm trees from here to the ocean, like you see today. There was no topsoil. I started composting right away with leaves, manure, sawdust, anything to build soil. I had a pickup truck and sought out materials for seven years to build soil. I have planted gardens and composted everywhere I have lived. This is a good place to grow. All the good land between my place and the ocean was sugar-cane fields at one time. Mexicanos dug the irrigation ditch, which is now piped. An old woman living in front of me said that as a young girl, she would bring lemonade to the workers who dug the ditch. The old, brick, two-story building down the road, which the locals call House of Dracula, was the headquarters for those cane fields.

I love my home. I used to have goats and chickens and a nice patch of raspberries. I harvest my big bamboo and share it. I have thirty-four fruit-bearing trees. I'm waiting for the *zapote negro* to ripen right now. There are Brazilian and Suriname cherries; pomelo, which is the grandfather of our modern grapefruit; Chilean guavas, sometimes called strawberry guavas because they are red; a blood-orange tree; *guanábana*; and several types of limes, lychee, date palms, and coconut palms.

MS. Tell me some stories about building this house.

JB. I had never built a house before, but I wanted to use straw bales. After I found a farmer with a baler, I measured his bales to make the right-size foundation. When I went to pick them up, he had changed balers, and they were smaller. Turns out it was a blessing, because that gave me room on the foundation for the cement siding. It took three years to build because I would go north for six months and care for my parents. I used the book *A Pattern Language* to design it and also fêng shui. I designed my entryway to bring in good chi for health and prosperity. To alter the chi of those who enter, there is a small pond with koi and a bridge people have to cross. When the fish got too big and multiplied, I would sell them to a pet store in La Paz. Now I have a submerged basket growing water lilies and a couple of waterfalls for sound chi.

Building it was a challenge and a learning experience. As soon as I had the roof on, my parents came down and slept on the couches. But there were no windows, and they froze. We arrived in the night. I opened the door and stepped on the floor, and my shoe stuck solid to the floor. The finish was an epoxy bond, and it was supposed to be done. But they had got the mix wrong, making it a gooey mess. There were dead geckos, cockroaches, and even a bird or two stuck to it.

My mother was well into Alzheimer's then, and she was right behind me, waiting to come in and lie down. What was I going to do? I got a roll of black garbage bags and rolled them out in a path to the bed, the bathroom, the kitchen, the doors. They stayed for eight weeks with the floor like that. I had to wait until they left to take out all the furniture and scrape it up and try again. The window guy never did put in the windows. I eventually had to take him to the state labor-arbitration office in La Paz to get him to finish. I partitioned off the kitchen and lived in there for a while. It's been an ongoing project.

In later years, I built a one-bedroom casita for my parents to live in. I used a lot of Mayan symbols in the cement walls and paths and sculpted Quetzalcoatl, the Mayan god of wisdom, along the top of the privacy wall. It has seen its share of life and is now home to a Mexican artist with a gallery in town. I also built a two-story casita with a healing center on the top floor and a small caretaker's quarters downstairs. It has been a blessing to be here.

MS. Healing center. Yes, let's talk about the book you wrote a few years back, the one I worked on.

JB. My dad had leukemia, and I didn't want to see him go through all the invasive treatments for cancer. So, I asked a doctor in Mexico City if I could study with him. Dr. Guiz is a genius who developed a healing method for over two hundred fifty diseases by normalizing the magnetic balance in the body. I went to Mexico City and studied with him. Later I translated the book that he had written about his findings and method. I was very excited about the work and would get up at four in the morning and translate all day. I sent him a copy, but he never responded. I kept working on it, improving everything, adding an index. When I saw him again, I asked if he didn't like it. He said, "Oh, no! I liked it. It's coming out next week!" He had published my rough draft! Here is the book right here. I told him I didn't want my name on it because it didn't include all the clarifications I had added to make it useable.

I started teaching classes in biomagnetic healing at the church here. The padre and the nuns were very supportive. A doctor in town tried to have me deported because I wasn't a citizen then and foreigners were restricted as to what they could and couldn't do, even for free. I am a citizen now. So, I stopped teaching and built the healing center here. I wrote a thesis on healing leukemia with biomagnetism and got a certificate for medical biomagnetism from the Universidad Autonoma Chipingo. It is the number-one university in Mexico dealing with the natural world. They have published volumes about all the healing plants of Mexico. After ten years of using Dr. Guiz's method, I wrote my own book explaining how to use his method, with lots of diagrams and pictures denoting placement of magnets. I included a thorough index to help readers locate information. I published it through Amazon's self-publishing program called CreateSpace in 2011. The book is called *Bioenergetic Basics*.

I see myself more as a teacher than a healer. I use the healing center for seminars because I think people can use this method to heal themselves. We all can heal ourselves using magnetism, herbs, stones, water, light, and sound and through contact with the earth. I believe we can learn to ask our bodies what we need and then can learn techniques to listen for the answer. We don't need to depend on healing coming always from the outside. I've benefitted from acupuncture, but what I really dislike is the pharmaceutical solution. I believe we can heal from what God has given us from the natural world.

During my life of travel, I have always bought rocks and stone beads and have quite the collection. I enjoy making healing jewelry with stone beads specific to healing the organs of the body—eyes, lungs, heart, and so on. The stones are constantly emitting a frequency vibration that corresponds to the body or mental or spiritual part of our existence.

MS. What do you see in the future for yourself?

JB. I want to simplify. I don't need a house this big. I would like to sell this one and live with fewer things. All I need is a bed, table, chairs, a light, a place to cook. I don't need all this stuff. Look at all this stuff! I've been selling books, clothes, furniture for the last few years. When I built this place, I thought it was simple! Counting

Casa Maya, the healing center, and caretaker's room, there are six bathrooms here! I want to sell the whole place."

MS. What have you learned about yourself living here?

JB. I'm still learning! I'm still on a quest for the next thing to learn. What I have learned is the depth of our world within us. I have been so focused on the outer. I've had many spiritual experiences in my life and in this house...miracles. Life is so precious. There is so much going on in the world; we can't predict what will happen next. We need to be aware of what's going on and be prepared, but we also need to pay attention to what's going on in the inside. Now my life seems really personal. I try to meditate every day. I don't want to spend so much time on the obstructions that come up on the outer, so many diversions that have no lasting meaning. All these things I have spent a lifetime doing, I'm not taking them with me.

MS. Seems to me you have integrated well with the Mexican culture. Your command of the language has opened lots of doors both here and on the mainland.

JB. Yes, that's true. Here is another book I contributed to: *Quien Es Quien en la Empresa a Mexico* [Who's Who in Mexican Business]. My sister married a Mexican and lives in Cuernavaca. In 1985, he helped me get a position to interview the successful businessmen of Mexico. I got to go into the beautiful mansions in Mexico City Here I have been involved in the town, the church, the music in La Paz.

MS. What about the challenges you have faced?

JB. Things have been challenging, but I have enjoyed everything I've done. They are more like adventures; do something, and see what happens. I love to learn. I went out with the fishermen to see what a shrimp boat was like. We climbed up the ladder into the boat and then down below where their freezers were. It was interesting and fascinating.

Hurricanes Juliet and Odile were challenging, all the cleanup both inside and outside in high heat. Lots of trees went down, and all my vehicles were damaged. I was exhausted, sick even, and couldn't afford to get away for a rest, what with all the expenses of cleanup and repair. I had a dinner party including racks of clothes, statues, books, and jewelry to give away: a big giveaway. At the end of the evening, I announced that I was going into retreat for a month right here in my own home, so, friends, don't call or come over. I'll call you if I need you. I needed to rest and meditate and take the pressure off.

On a positive note, I am challenging myself to meditate every day. Also, I'm trying to practice two-prong attention, which I learned about from Gurdjieff a while back. While dealing with the outside world, you remain conscious of your inner self. Sort of like mindfulness. I find I have to speak and move slower in the world to do this.

Janice had helped me in La Paz to jump through hoops to become a legal business. At one point they wanted some paper verifying something, and they were about to close. Janice said, "I know where that office is; let's take a cab so we don't have to walk back to the car." We dashed there and back in time. Another time it was something similar, and never did she say no. She always said, "Let's go!" My impression of her was her positive attitude, a can-do dynamism.

MS. Is there something in your past that endowed you with the confidence and self-esteem it takes to accomplish the tasks you have undertaken?

JB. Being raised Mormon, at age twelve, I received a patriarchal blessing, sort of a guidance for your life ceremony. I was told that my strength was that whatever my heart desired, I could accomplish. That was very positive, and I must have taken it to heart. Mormonism had some shortfalls, though. When I was five, I looked at my father's scrapbook of when he traveled widely as a Mormon missionary. He went to India, China, and Japan and spent three years in Africa. Women were encouraged to stay home and have babies. I remember thinking, "It's not fair. I know God loves me, but why did he make me a woman?" Later when I could be a missionary in Chile, I jumped at the chance. I've been a feminist since age five. I had to come to grips with being a woman on an inner level.

MS. How much time do you spend on the computer?

JB. Not as much as I used to, because it is hard for me to read. I have macular degeneration, which is another reason I don't play music anymore. After three years of acupuncture and eating for my eyes and wearing stones for healing the eyes, they are better. I was able to pass my driver's test. That has been a challenge. I still research online, but it is difficult. I look at it as a blessing, because it is forcing me to spend more time on my inner life. The time I used to spend playing music or researching is now freed up for meditating.

MS. With your vast connection to the Mexican people, are there traits that you admire?

JB. Their freedom.

MS. Freedom from what?

JB. They don't have the hang-ups that we do. They're more free. We're all in cultural boxes, but I see they are not in the same boxes I'm in. For example, Americans are afraid of government regulations, and down here they just sort of dance around them. There's the story of the business man who tells the fisherman he should have a bigger boat, work longer hours, and make more money so he can relax under the palm tree when he retires. And the fisherman says, "I relax under the palm tree now." I also like that in Mexico, Sunday is family day and the family is together that day. You see large family groupings on the beach under umbrellas and tents, with barbecue units, or in the cities, tables out on the sidewalk because the house is crowded with family. They are definitely not in the box of having a skinny body to be beautiful!

MS. Are you ever afraid here?

JB. I'm afraid of mice! Maybe it's just that I don't like them. When I lived in Chile, which was a real third-world country, I developed habits of security, like locking the gate and the house even when I'm out in the yard. It was in the sixties, with revolutions happening; we had bars on the windows. Here I built the wall outside to have more privacy in my outdoor living space. The bars on these windows are diamond shaped and small to resemble my grandmother's lead windowpanes. If the window pane or bars are smaller than a head, a person cannot enter through them.

I feel protected, so I am not afraid. The world situation is frightening, what with chemtrails poisoning the atmosphere, so I like to know what is happening but then investigate ways of mitigating the effects. For example, coffee enemas to stimulate the liver and gallbladder to eliminate toxins that seem prevalent nowadays. I ask my body everyday what it needs. You have to shut off the left brain, and then you're in your real self. We have a spark of divinity in us, which is a way of knowing the truth. We can all know the truth. What is going on in the body is just a part of that. I also ask what my dog needs. I am keeping her young by asking what she needs daily and then giving it to her. You can also ask your plants what they need.

MS. Is there any advice you would like to pass on to the readers of this book?

JB. Follow your star, your inner knowing. A lot of us were brought down here by that process. The decision wasn't mental but an inspiration.

Janice had just taken me on a trip around the world, through the arts, healing, growing food, writing books. She stood by her ethics through it all. Janice, you are an inspiration about following your star.

CHAPTER 4
DIANE JOY

I first met Diane when she was living in Elias Calle, a tiny town without much of a center, more a wide spot in the road, with a very distinctive old brick building right by the road. It had been spared from demolition by the road-widening crew as they turned Baja Highway 19 into a divided four-lane road from Todos Santos to Cabo San Lucas. It is a much safer road, and I, personally, was glad that the old building didn't have to go. My son actually designed a house in Todos Santos based on the proportions of that old place. I wonder when the building was built and what its function was.

Before I got a laptop, I would go to a narrow, *zaguan* [hallway, alleyway], Internet-access place next to the Todos Santos Cafe, one of the first gringo owned restaurants in town. Diane was a neighbor at the next computer, and I sensed that I could share a heartwarming YouTube short with her. I did, and she started to tear up. She had blue, sparkling eyes and a mischievous smile. I liked her. We talked and soon became friends.

She had just arrived on the Pacific side of the peninsula after spending a year in La Paz helping a friend of a friend open a restaurant. She returned to the United States to have surgery on her shoulder. Too many years of doing therapeutic massage took its toll. She said, "I came back to Baja because it's *not cold*, for one thing, and I can live on my social-security check because I am frugal. I didn't want to live in La Paz. It was too hot, and the part of town where I lived didn't have the cleanest air."

The day of the interview was bright and sunny and the air was clean. I had invited her out to my house because she likes my house and her apartment is too crowded, cramped and cluttered for my sensibilities. She has crammed a life, a bakery, a boyfriend, two dogs and a cat in a tiny apartment. That day Diane was dressed in a yellow, possibly Indian-import, muumuu type of tie-dyed affair, which was perfect for the weather and her full body. We shared a cup of tea as we talked about this major life transition late in her life…moving to Mexico.

MS. What was your family's reaction to your decision to come to Mexico?

Diane Joy (DJ). I'm crazy, as usual. It was unsafe, they told me. I'm from New York City! They said it wasn't safe for me to drive four thousand miles by myself. My car was packed so tightly you couldn't get a tooth pick in it. [*When she returned to Baja after the shoulder surgery, she came with a friend, Debbie, towing a trailer of Debbie's stuff.*] Baja Highway One is not an easy drive, but Debbie was making it worse by reacting hysterically to the hills and curves in the mountainous areas. We rented a little house in Elias Calle, without any electricity. It wasn't the best location, because it was a long way to anywhere. Debbie eventually felt like she was allergic to Baja and went back home. She coughed all the time.

MS. Did you have any expectations of the move?

DJ. None. If I had thought about it long and hard, I might not have come, but I knew I couldn't support myself in the States anymore with no massage income from the crippled-up shoulders. I couldn't afford my rent, which was almost the amount of my social-security check. I was just looking for a place to live. I wanted to live in Italy or Sicily, but, no, I don't think I'll be traveling anymore at my age. I eventually moved to Todos Santos, a bigger small town.

When I asked Diane, "How was that move?" she jumped right to making a living.

DJ. I tried doing massage again, but there are a lot of massage therapists here who come to your home. I'm seventy-six now, and schlepping the massage table around is not for me. So I cooked and baked instead. [*She had a big, proud smile.*] I'm the Pie Lady!

DJ. I started off baking pies. Everyone loves pies. Not many places to sell pies, though, so I did the farmer's markets, which were fun and friendly. It was my social life. I became known as the Pie Lady. But it was a lot of schlepping, and if they didn't sell, I ate a lot of pie. I'm really a reclusive person, and when people see me on the street and recognize me and call out, "The Pie Lady!" I feel uncomfortable. It's a small town. I also catered Thanksgiving and Christmas dinners and made food for some of the elder gentlemen in town. It was costly and required a lot of checking in with the clientele.

As Diane and I went on, I got a whole manual on the experience of the economics of turning a talent for cooking into pesos for life. It could be titled *Harder to Cook Than Bake*.

DJ. Then I found a great recipe for carrot cake. Now there are two stores that buy my carrot cakes of the perfect size, and it is an uncomplicated, once or twice a week, half day's work. It's a good supplementary income, which fuels my love of eating out in this town of restaurants. [*The two stores, by the way, are !Que Rico! and Puro Vida. They are the perfect size because of the beach lifestyle here, little loaves to share and eat in a day.*]

Diane lived now in one of the smallest apartments I had seen anyone live in, except maybe the chick renting the walk-in closet in San Francisco. Aside from a bedroom, which is mostly bed, and a bathroom, it was all kitchen. Kitchen stuff on wire racks, kitchen counters, one of which was made of cement and was "perfect for rolling out pie dough because it is cold," and one with a cutting board. Diane said that she took the place because it had a big refrigerator and a big oven. There was a table with three hazardous chairs clustered around it and a computer table.

"My tiny space is getting tinier by the day," Diane said as she made a sad face.

Diane moved four times in the five years she had been in Todos Santos before settling here on a wide, dusty street in Barrio San Vicente. She said, "I feel safe here behind a locked gate and protected by three surrounding houses, which shielded me from the big hurricane last fall, a category three-four direct hit. I have never been so scared in my life!"

I admire the emigrant women I've met here who have had to move multiple times…all that stuff! No matter what we come with, we tend to buy the beautiful Mexican art and fabrics sold in the town and at the regional art shows. Not so, Diane. I always admired her elder wisdom as I saw her choices of what she brought down. Mainly tools of her trade, small and not-so-small appliances, raw craft materials, and a favorite Tiffany lampshade. She said she also brought lace curtains, but they got away from her in one of the moves.

When I asked her how much she lived on per month, the answer was a confident $500. For rent, $300, and the rest for electric, propane, and food. Hard to believe, considering what I knew of her eating-out habit. She winked and said, "I never figured it out because I'm mathlexic."

MS. Do you feel like you have integrated into the Mexican community?

DJ. No, not at all. I'm a hermit really and can't communicate in their language. I'm not a Mexican.

MS. Do you speak Spanish now?

DJ. A little bit. The gardener who comes here is very helpful and friendly, but I can't understand a word he says because he has no teeth. Spanish without teeth, I can't understand it.

MS. What would you say about the Mexican culture?

DJ. They are very friendly, never say no, and I'm beginning to catch on to the mañana mentality. Sometimes they say they will be there to fix something, and they never show up, never call. But, yeah, "mañana" is good enough to say when you don't really know when you'll be back.

MS. Do you feel safe here?

DJ. I do. I'm tucked in at the back of the lot. My garbage pail has been stolen outside the gate, but that's all.

MS. Have you learned any major life lessons while you have lived here?

DJ. A big one is, nothing matters!

With this, Diane pressed her outstretched hands on the table and lowered her head as if challenging the universe to confront her decision.

DJ. Nothing can come into my life to make me unhappy. I won't allow it. I was severely depressed in the United States. When I got here, I stopped taking my meds and have been fine ever since. I am probably one of those people who need sunshine. [*There is a lot of that down here. Just open your eyes, and you are surrounded by sweet light, gentle ocean breezes, and friendly people.*] I'm happy because I have a wonderful life, people are loving and kind, and I'm healthy and get around. I have met incredible women in Todos Santos.

MS. Was it easy to make friends here?

DJ. No. It is never easy for me to make friends. I'm different. Some women might feel intimidated by me. I'm gregarious but also shy. I notice that when I'm in a crowd, I hardly speak. I've nothing to say.

MS. Do you ever get bored or lonely?

DJ. Bored, yes, but momentarily. Not lonely.

MS. I know you have been quite consistent in attending the Dharma Talk on Sundays. Say something about that.

DJ. While living in Elias Calle, I saw a picture of Robert Hall in a magazine. [*Robert is a meditation teacher from the United States who has lived in Todos Santos for many years and shares a weekly dharma talk to a full house during the tourist season, winter, and to devotees the rest of the year*] I fell instantly in love with him and said "I have to meet this man." The influence of Buddhism, as taught by Robert Hall, has changed my life significantly. I am so much calmer and not so angry. I have gone almost every Sunday since I have been here.

MS. What about your love life? Any?

With a big sigh and shy smile, Diane told me about having her astrology chart done upon a recommendation of a friend. She said, "It was spot-on: 'You don't have to go looking for love. It will come knocking at your door.' Hurricane Odile scared the hell out of me. It was the first time I felt really alone. There I was, sitting with my babies, my dogs, Canela and Lucky, pressed into my armpits, terrified. I said a prayer: 'Oh, please, goddess, send someone to love me.' That was a different prayer for me. I used to always pray for someone to love. After Odile, I got really sick for the first time in years. Maybe I had pneumonia.

"This guy I had known for a while came knocking at my door. He took care of me, nursed me back to health, schlepped for me. That was six months ago, and he's still here! Now I have a companion, helper, nudnick, another crazy gringo. He's a surfer and fifty-five! That's twenty years younger than me! I'm a cougar! I ask him, 'What do you see in this old woman?' He replies, 'You're not old, and I really love you.' And I deserve it. No one has ever loved me before."

I can testify to their loving relationship. They like to talk and listen to each other and appreciate each other's humor. Diane's face is more serene, and her whole demeanor is calmer and sweeter. He helps make the carrot cakes and takes them to the surfing beaches to sell to a hungry and appreciative crowd. It's working out for them both. They recently drove up to the States to retrieve his motor home from his mother's backyard. Now it sits in the double-wide parking area inside the gate so that they can have more room than the tiny apartment offers.

MS. Any future plans, Diane?

DJ. Want to make God laugh? Make a plan. He-he. I just know I couldn't move back to the United States and live, unless, God forbid, I should get sick or need surgery. I would not have it done here. I don't want to live with my daughter in her house. She comes down here once a year and likes it. I'm a happy camper.

MS. What are some of your favorite restaurants in the area?

DJ. I like the baby back ribs at Chill and Grill and the Asian food at Rumi's Garden. Your readers can have fun eating out here when they get here!

Now there's an incentive to check it out!

CHAPTER 5

JANEL BEEMAN

I had to step over a small hill of dirt to get to Janel's gate. Her street was one of many in Todos Santos in the process of being paved. Lots of leveling and grading was leaving piles of dirt in unexpected places. By this time the dog had sensed my presence and had sounded the alarm: "Visitor!"

Janel soon appeared and gave Teo the settle sign. As I came in the gate, I was shown the new gatepost. Quite handsome and sturdy looking. My own gate just got three new hinges to help the last remaining one hold my scene together, so I appreciated the maintenance efforts of the householder.

Because it was already hot, we ducked quickly into Janel's cozy casita—everything you need in a four-hundred-square-foot house. Janel went over to the computer where Amy Goodman's voice was sounding good sense and turned it off. I asked her, "Do you listen to Amy Goodman every morning?"

She responded, "Most mornings."

After checking out the screened-in porch that she had added a few years back (one I always liked because it was big enough to handle big projects) and sharing a glass of freshly made green drink, we got to the questions of why, how, and what else?

Janel Beeman (JB). Usually where I hang out is below the threshold of daily thoughts; "deeper truths" are maybe words for it. In my early years, there came up a habit of being hypervigilant about everything. It was a survival mechanism I developed, which allowed me to see things that other people don't. It made relationships more difficult, because you don't want to see these things; you want to be more accepting and allow flow to happen. The positive side was seeing beneath the threshold of daily life. The Western cultures are almost fanatically surface oriented. To think below the surface is to embody spirit rather than believe in spirit.

I had been having spontaneously erupting, psychic experiences, which changed my whole belief structure of what life is all about. My husband was supportive, though he was a scientist at NASA. He was very interested in what was going on with me, but he was also jealous because he wished to have experiences like that. He went off to Brazil to ingest psychedelic plants with the Indians, and he came back with a woman who was the age I was when we originally got together.

It was appropriate. I knew things had to change, but I didn't want to. I was safe and secure. He took care of a lot of stuff I didn't want to do and was supportive. We moved to Idaho that winter and lived five miles from the nearest neighbor, where we parked the car and skied or snowmobiled in. Sometimes he would be gone for weeks, and I was with myself, attuning to the emanations from physical things until it got to the point where I could tell within my body the location of every moose and bear. Previously I had spent two years alone in the high sierras of California, fifteen miles away from the nearest neighbors. That is where I first heard my own voice on all levels. Then he returned home with the young lady.

He had never loved Latin cultures. I had been a Latin American–studies major at one time and loved Latin cultures. I had traveled in Mexico a lot because my dad had an airplane, and we would fly down to spend a summer in Mexico City. I also traveled in Mexico by myself, at one time living a whole year in a village in Oaxaca as a young, blond woman.

The day our divorce mediation ended, I left on a woman's kayaking trip on Magdalena Bay, Baja California Sur. After a week of wonder in that country, I looked on the map and saw Loreto and Todos Santos. I liked the name Todos Santos and came down. I spent two weeks as a guest of Jane Perkins, who had started the El Tecolote Book Store and became my mentor here.

I had never had a mentor before. She did a good job when she saw that I was interested in staying. She took me around and pointed out architecture and styles of living. She showed me this neighborhood but never told me how many difficulties she had in a similar neighborhood. I do love this neighborhood, in spite of the ten dogs down the block and all the traffic. I'm solitary and single. But life goes on around me, so I feel part of it. I'm really happy here and happy in Todos Santos.

MS. Did you feel at the time that you were going to relocate here?

JB. I had been to La Paz when I was twelve with my father, in 1950. I wanted to see more of Baja. In 1996, I was at loose ends, and it was good timing. I decided to make a reservation with Jane for three months starting in December. In the meantime, I went back to Oregon and sold two houses and every stick of furniture in them. We had to divide up our stuff. It was a lot of work! Then I went to Oregon and moved my mother out of her house.

When I got back to Todos Santos, I didn't ever want to see another house and any stuff! It was ten days before I visited the realtor whom I had talked to previously and told her I wasn't interested in buying a house. She said the price on a half-acre lot had been dropped by half and that I should walk by it and take a look. I did, ate three pomegranates growing on that land, walked back to the office, and bought it. I bought these two lots first and then later bought the lot on the other side of the arroyo. It was owned by Lorna, or Lorena, a gringa who married a Mexican and went to his home in Candelaria in the mountains east of here. She was instrumental in reviving pottery in that small town. There she lives to this day without another gringa in sight. These two lots I bought from Lee Moore, who lived here twenty-five years before moving to La Paz. So within three weeks of being back, I was in the process of building. That was in 1996.

MS. So much for simplifying and taking a break. As the song says, "When a big wind comes your way, be ready to sail." So how was the building experience?

JB. I never thought about building. I had remodeled the cabin in Idaho but never built from the ground up. I had good support, and it was well done. I had a great contractor: a longtime resident, Patrick Coffman. He drew up the plans and knew things I would never have thought of. Memo was the builder. He was a handsome guy. We had coffee every morning. And if you have to look at people every morning, it's nice if they are that pretty and that smart! He was thoughtful and a lot of fun. He was macho, too. ["*Macho,*" *according to my dictionary, is, among other things, "vigorous and strong." It has also been said that "a macho" is a protector.*]

I started with that house in the corner. It has a very big bedroom because there were eight workers living on the land building the place, and I had no private place to do yoga. [*It should work well for a Mexican family, who might put four or five beds in that one big room.*] It took two years to finish all three houses and the apartment.

MS. Two years! That's really fast!

JB. I have always been one to get things done. It's an attribute and an undoing, because I don't think things through enough. It's a double-edged sword. And I had fantasies.

MS. You did?

We both had a laugh. As I've watched people come here, I have seen that they are all living some kind of dream or fantasy.

JB. I raised five children, and the fantasy was that my sons would come down and live in the two houses whenever they had the chance. It has not been the case.

What Janel said was familiar to me. I have seen this mistake more than once out where I live. People build these huge houses so that their children will come and occupy all the rooms, and they hardly ever come. They have their own lives and careers and vacation choices besides Mom's place in southern Baja.

JB. Actually it was a good thing, and I'm grateful, because I never really had much independence. I was married at nineteen and had my first child nine months and one week after that.

My family was into Western medicine, and being the rebellious child, I went into Chinese medicine. I had a career in traditional Chinese medicine in Palo Alto and led women's wilderness retreats in the Sierra Nevada Mountains. I hated being in an office. I loved the wilderness retreats and saw that people were empowered and healed more deeply from that experience than with the Chinese medicine. From these experiences, I learned the necessity of balance and taking total responsibility for my own health.

MS. Well, as a mother of five, you were juggling twenty-five things with two hands, a head, and a heart. Talk about balance!

JB. It has been an unusual life. Each of my children spent time with me as an only child. I have made so many mistakes, giant mistakes in my life! My kids would come to me and say, "I gotta tell ya something, Mom." After hearing, I would respond, "Oh, that is nothing. I have done so much worse!" Right now my parents aren't watching me, nor are my children. I'm unsupervised! Not having to meet anyone's expectations.

MS. Well, you certainly took on a huge responsibility here.

JB. I'm a Leo and have so much fire and air in my astrological chart that it took five kids to ground me, and they taught me how to love. This place also grounded me. We were reviewed in a most elegant way in the *New York Times*. That came after eight years of offering rentals. The next year they made one of the adjacent roads a cargo route for the semis to use to avoid the downtown area, and that destroyed the business.

MS. That's unfortunate.

JB. No, it wasn't. I was tired of the rental scene by then. The lot has an arroyo through it, which was never problematical even in the 2001 hurricane. It has only been in the last four years that the property has seemed too much for me. I'm seventy-seven this year. I have lived in all three houses and the apartment, which is good because I get to fine-tune them. I was busy building from 1996 to 1998, in a time when wiring money took weeks because it would get lost.

MS. How did you get customers?

JB. I did all the normal things. I had a website, cards, and brochures around town and an ad in Trip Advisor, and I made sure all the satisfied guests commented on their stay in Trip Advisor. In 2007, the year before the cargo route impacted the serenity of the place, we were rated the number-one place to stay in Todos Santos by Trip Advisor. The surprise to me was that I really enjoyed the people who came here. The ad mentioned yoga, meditation, opportunities to participate with the Internado [*the housing for rancho kids who stay all week in town for school and return to the rancho on the weekend*], and a smoke-free environment, so it was self-selected. Those who came, about ninety percent of them, I could genuinely care about.

But then the town routed big trucks this way without paving, and the dust was hideous. They gave me no warning, so I had gone ahead with advertising. I had visitors from Venezuela and New York, and you couldn't see across the street because of the dust. I had to find them other places and reimburse them. I lost *all my savings* in two years. I left here with my blood pressure sixty-forty. I fainted on the way to the doctor. That was after a night in which three of the big orange machines worked until one in the morning, with the drivers screaming dirty jokes to each other.

I had to sell my car to pay off my employees. I left with two thousand dollars and no idea where another cent was coming from. It was a big shock to not be in business anymore, but it was also a relief. The words in the *Times* article described it as "immaculately groomed, park-like surroundings," so for years, I had been going around picking up every leaf that had fallen.

I went to New Mexico and stayed with some young friends, but later I went to visit a friend more my age, who introduced me to her friends, who were all odd, elder women. Yeah! It was a mountain community. A tiny lot I owned in Pescadero sold and gave me enough money to buy a car. I rented a little cabin right next to a creek—hammock in place. I had a great time there not owning. I had time for solitude and helped to start a sustainability group, which is still going on and is now a nonprofit organization. Also I helped to start a fiber-arts workshop, which had classes, and we tried to figure out selling schemes. I wrote for the local paper and had a lot of fun. I don't do those things when I'm settled, because there's too much responsibility, with all of everything needed to run this place and keep it up.

Of course the money started to run out. I had had one late bill in all my life. I started to live on credit cards. It was a huge struggle, having never done that before. My spiritual guidance was telling me that I was not supposed to be thinking about money *at all.* I have learned over the years to trust that guidance. There was a conflict in my conditioning about living on credit cards and what I was being told to do by my guidance. Self-correction and learning inner independence are the essence of my spiritual work. I didn't know when to leave and what to do. At what point do you start living on the street?

Guidance said it was not my concern and that I should stay in the present moment. The caretaker here had communicated to me that her fisherman husband wasn't doing so good and that they were going to have to leave. I had to come home. The credit card paid for my last tank of gas in San Diego, and by then, all the credit cards were maxed out. I loved it actually. I had no other choices. I drove home to Todos Santos with some cash in my pocket and several hundred dollars in a Mexican bank to start again. My car was stuffed, one shoe at a time.

JB. The next three years were hell. My limits stretched to where I couldn't stand it. The cargo route got paved, and the traffic of big trucks was so loud that you couldn't have a conversation. When you can't stand it anymore, your limits change. My feelings were really foul when I got back. There were so many dogs across the street. There were thirty piles of dog shit outside my gate every morning for me to move.

As soon as I changed my thoughts, there were one or two piles. I know how to do internal work. You work with it until you come to genuine gratitude. It's tedious and difficult, and it takes you to your limits. I had felt that the pueblo had violated me and the kids in the school nearby. They didn't care. They cared about the tourists in *el centro* [downtown]. This was the scene for three years until they made the bypass outside of town instead of in front of my house and holdings.

MS. How do you feel now about the responsibility of being the *dueña?*

JB. Seven of the nine dogs moved away; the screaming neighbor lady on the other side moved away. The neighborhood has changed a little. It is much quieter. Catastrophe is an essential part of spiritual life, because it breaks down your conditioning. Life was getting better, and then Odile hit. [*Gasp!*]

MS. How was Odile for you?

JB. Thirty-five palms down, three *palapa* roofs damaged, almost all the fences down, and I had three hundred pesos total. I lost almost every structure. There was not one thing on the property that was not affected. A friend arrived and gave me one thousand pesos. My kids got some money together for me, and eventually

I was able to give one thousand pesos to the woman who lives in the dump as a payback to humanity. I had to wait almost a year to clean up the mess in the road [*palms dragged there by the cleanup crew*]. I felt like I was defiling the neighborhood. Luckily for me, another lot in Pescadero sold. I might have holes in my clothes, but eighty percent of the work here is now done a year later.

MS. Well, that all builds character.

JB. There's been big catastrophes in my life before I came here, but with Odile, I was knocked off balance. I did recover more quickly than in the past and never missed a day of yoga and meditation. I was able to center and be grateful for the food I ate every day. I had a car and a safe place to be and clothes on my back.

Being able to focus on real gratitude, not just Pollyanna-style, has healed me more than Chinese medicine, and it comes through meditation. I once went to a meditation retreat that was eleven hours a day sitting meditation. It was like major surgery, but it worked. Mostly I meditate by myself now. Three times a year, I go to the Dzogchen Gar in the Sierras for five to seven days to be by myself and meditate. They have nice cabins separate from each other, and two meals are served a day. You can participate in their events if you want, but I go to meditate by myself.

Janel was referring to Dzogchen, one of the great spiritual traditions of Tibet. Tsegyalgar West is land donated to the Dzogchen community of Southern Baja as a space for personal and group retreats. Chogyal Namkhai Norbu is a contemporary Dzogchen master who visits the site and gives direct transmissions, which are at the very heart of the teachings. For more information, see www.tsegyalgarwest.org.

MS. So why have you stayed?

JB. I'm big-time invested in this property. Aside from my children, it is the one thing I have not been able to walk away from. I have to stay and face it. Meditation is like that. You have to sit with yourself.

MS. What are some of the lessons you have learned from your experience?

JB. Through all of what I would describe as hell, discomfort, and poverty, I have lost my unconscious entitlement that we gringos arrive with. Living close to poverty shows me my excesses on a daily basis. I wrote a poem. Its whole tone is not beautiful and sophisticated, more like what Mexico is.

> Black cat, splat flat.
> Dead toad in the road.
> Dog shit underfoot.
> Broken glass under tire.
> Septic seeping smell.
> How is it I got here? I forget.
> Fourteen girls walking with their arms around each other's shoulders.
> Brown boy leans down to comfort baby sister.
> Adult mother and daughter walking hand in hand.
> Ah, now I begin to remember.
> Mexico is too loud, too dusty, too raw.
> Looks like I'm going to stay.

MS. Thanks for sharing. That is the first poem in the interviews. What about the future?

JB. I feel like the place is all too big for me and would like to bring it down in scale. With what is planned across the street, this will be the secondary commercial center of town. [*The Tres Santos development across the street from one of her fence lines includes a branch of Colorado State University and condos, houses, a shopping center, and bike trails to the ocean. The entire plan carries the threat of tripling the size of the town.*] I would like to sell half this place, the arroyo being the dividing line, or have a couple of older women live here and own their place and share some of the responsibility in a corporation. To have long-term renters, I would have to really like them.

I am content right now and am not moving on any plan. I would be interested in anyone who wanted to come and feel out participation in this place. I take orders from my guidance and absolutely trust them. Our culture teaches us to push forward, make it happen, sometimes force things. It's different from being ready to receive, being present, and letting things happen. One thing I've learned from the Mexicans is a gentleness of spirit and to let time and spirit unfold the situation.

MS. Do you feel like you have integrated with the Mexican culture?

JB. My experience is always changing, because I have been here for nineteen years. Sometimes I speak more Spanish than English and then the reverse. I like both. At parties, they are so solicitous to make me comfortable that it makes everyone else uncomfortable. I don't have perfect Spanish, so I miss a lot at big parties. I went to Oaxaca three summers to language school and came back here with more fluency and a greater vocabulary. But here the people are poorly educated, and I don't use what I have learned. I've learned from my employees. They have a way of negotiating without conflict or great pressure. They are gentle and diplomatic, and everyone feels good at the end of the talk. There are other ways to negotiate than the way we were taught to confront.

MS. How do you live with all these challenges?

JB. Learning acceptance, learning that adversity is what renders off the fat. I've put in request for a different outcome, like chocolate bonbons, but it hasn't happened.

MS. What do you do with your time?

JB. I write. Since Odile, I have been writing. Surface reality is an everyday event, but the writing helps me go deeper and keep what is mine. I am writing about the spiritual adventures of my life.

I don't know what its future is—publishing or not. I am enjoying the process. I am up at five in the morning to meditate and exercise and then gallivant with Teo in the hills and by the ocean, every day a different place. Then I study the mystery, all those things that are not visible in ordinary life: the I Ching, taro, animal cards, soul cards. They are gateways to intuition, below face value. I do holiday cooking. I enjoy a small slice of social life. My life is the same wherever I am. If I'm getting bored, it's because I'm not going deep enough.

MS. Does your family come down?

JB. Two of them have never come down; they are deep in their careers. My younger son has come down twice. It's been a stretch, but I've learned more inner independence. Throughout my life, I have been funneled to a one-pointed dedication to spirit, and so every bit of stretching has been the magic I get to experience. Now I just say, "OK, whatever needs to be done." It is so magical. It's been shown to me that I need to ground to get higher in the spiritual experience.

MS. Do you ever get bored and lonely?

JB. Sure, but those are part of the growth path of elders.

MS. What do you think about the changes in Todos Santos now?

JB. I think it is for tourism. I don't know who it is benefiting. It's a transitional time. There are negatives and positives about the Tres Santos development. There was black, septic water running in the street, and for ten days, we wrestled with the water department. Then I wrote to Ernie, part of the Mira Corporation. He sent four guys down to the water department, and it was fixed that day. I have complained about other things to him. Any kind of big change frightens people. Someday the coastline from here to San Diego will be developed, so you might as well have a good developer. It's bigger than I am. I have fought environmental battles before, and now I pick and choose which ones I fight for.

MS. Is there anything you would like the readers to know?

JB. This is a horrible thing to bring up, but I have had two gringa friends murdered here. Don't be gaga and miss reality. Things happen here like everywhere else. If you come to buy property, rent first so that you know where you want to live, so that you know what is going on. In the end, how do you know? We change as we live here. I have no regrets. The whole situation demands that I stay engaged. My income demands it. So I am, and I love it.

CHAPTER 6

WENDY RAINS

Wendy's entry was scented with jasmine flowers on the trimmed tree in the middle of the courtyard. I had to pause to sniff them. The door opened, and there were Wendy and two big, elderly dogs happy to see a visitor. She was dressed in a vibrantly colored, print sundress of modern style and design, and her eyelids were painted to match all three colors. It was meticulously done; she was a woman who knew how to display her fine features, beautiful soft brown, eyes and wide smile. She was the poster girl for sixty-seven being the new forty-five.

The house was an open-plan, one-story structure with large rooms and lots of furniture and art. We went to the big kitchen and got some orange water for refreshment. Seated at the large round table, we began to talk about when she brought her father, Eddie, who was then eighty-one, to Todos Santos in 2002 for an R and R break from the caretaking of his wife and Wendy's mother, who had dementia.

Wendy had been considering Costa Rico, when a friend suggested that they go to Todos Santos in the lower Baja. The friend was partners in a one-hundred-acre chili farm six miles out of town and maintained an apartment in town for her trips to administer the business. She offered them the apartment to stay in. Neither of them had been to Todos Santos although they had been to Cabo San Lucas many times. They found the apartment comfortable and clean, in spite of having to pass beer cans on the stairway leading up to it. Wendy and her father were used to much finer, more elegant digs, but that first night the most beautiful, soulful singing and guitar strumming wafted up from the floor below, where the workers gathered to pick up their weekly pay. This was a magical moment that had both Wendy and her dad charmed by the quaint, tiny town.

That first night they went looking for and found the Cafe Santa Fe, an Italian cuisine restaurant that put Todos Santos on the map. For many years, Cafe Santa Fe had been serving elegant meals to all who made a special trip to Todos Santos just to eat there.

The next morning in search of breakfast, Wendy shouted across the street to the first gringo she saw, "Hey, where can we eat?"

"Follow me," came the reply from the realtor they would soon work with. He led them to the Cafe Todos Santos, another early gringo entrepreneurial endeavor, which is still quietly sitting beneath luscious bougainvillea vines in the historic section of town. Actually, the café is on the first main street of town, which is narrow, not designed for cars and trucks, and usually festooned with traditional cutout *banderas* [flags] Along this street are also the fine big houses of the early settlers who profited from the sugar cane business in early Todos Santos. I so enjoyed Wendy's memory of her first impression of the Café.

Wendy Rains (WR) When I stepped in the door and saw the murals on the walls, the carved Spanish bench, the framed art on the walls, the tattooed biker who was the owner...everything, I asked myself, 'Where am I?' There was an air of sophistication mixed with old-world culture in a charming, historic setting that enticed me toward a new adventure at a time when I hadn't yet realized that was what I was craving. I had every intention of staying in the LA area, but falling in love with Todos Santos changed all that. When I told Dad how I felt and that I could live here, he said, 'So could I!' So we immediately started looking for a property we could share."

MS. You're not a small-town girl. What was it that kindled this fire?

WR. I was fifty-four years old at the time and had been separated from my husband for four years. I was fifty; my kids were grown, and I left my husband of twenty-one years to start a life of my own. My ex-husband has a record label and manages recording artists. When we met, I was thrust into that life and helped him get started. We had raised our kids on the road with bands and entertainers. My own career was thriving at the same time as well. I was a successful interior designer, having had offices in LA, Dallas, New Orleans, and later New York. We had homes in Malibu, Manhattan, and Steamboat Springs, Colorado...surrounded by lots of help... quite a cushy life. I was very much ready for a simpler life.

My mother's parents were Russian emigrants, and my grandfather developed a lot of northern New Jersey in the forties through the sixties. My mom was a designer, and she and my dad had us moving to new homes and towns all the time. Every winter from November to April until I was sixteen was spent in Miami Beach. My father homeschooled my sister and me, which was very rare in those days.

They moved us to Brentwood, California, when I was sixteen, starting the eleventh grade, and for the first time, I went full-time to a regular school. I moved every two years with my birth family. My parents built so many houses; I was raised on blueprints. This is the longest I have lived in one place...thirteen years. So you see, even though I knew not one word of Spanish, I had no fear of building a house, even in a foreign country.

While living in LA, I would go to the California desert by myself once a month for three days to unwind. I felt a similarity to my favorite escape here in Todos Santos, and I wanted to be someplace close to my kids. Two weeks after our initial visit, I came down and found this land. It was big enough that we could each have a home and privacy, share a pool and guesthouse, and have lots of land to garden and grow food. We bought it directly from the farmer—no haggling, just gave him what he wanted.

We designed our homes and hired a reliable builder who spoke English. I came down once a month for three days to check on things. At that time I was executive director for the nonprofit Ballona Wetlands Foundation, responsible for restoring the last and largest wetlands in LA County. Funding was running out for my position, so the timing was perfect for me to gracefully orchestrate my exit from LA. I was able to engage Loyola Marymount University to take over all my programs, which resulted in their creating an environmental affairs department.

MS. How did you find the building process in Baja Sur?

WR. Pretty painless. I was lucky with my builder. The finished house is not exactly as I envisioned it. But I did have a fêng shui consultant go over my plans, so everything has been built according to what would be most auspicious for me. I moved into the house the day of my first hurricane, Marty, with one hundred forty miles an hour wind and horizontal rain flooding the house while seven guys were trying to bring everything inside. No electricity or services back then. Quite an initiation!

MS. How many hurricanes have you lived through?

WR. Four, but moving day and last year's Odile were the two worst. Odile was my dad's first hurricane down here.

MS. How is that, living by your father?

There was silence, and then Wendy let out a big laugh. She said, "He gives me lots of material. I've been writing a blog for Eldersense.com, Alternative Aging in Place, about being a senior citizen myself, living on the same property with my ninety-four-year-old father in a foreign country. He has been living here full-time for five years now and really loves it. I am so glad to be able to provide a magical way for him to spend his last years after living such an incredible life."

MS. What are some of the lessons you have learned here?

WR. The first answer that comes to mind is patience. I never realized how impatient I was until I moved here. I had always been a snap decision-maker and action taker. I'd never tolerate someone not showing up for an appointment or taking forever to return a phone call or someone moving too slowly doing a task. People here say yes to everything because they don't want to disappoint you, but then they don't show or call to say they aren't coming. I could write a book on the excuses I've heard. They're comical! Now I can laugh about it. It's taken a while, but I have truly learned how to slow down and just know that everything will work itself out. When I go back to LA or any city, I can be stopped at a red light for longer than usual and not get crazy. Now I get crazy from the sensory overload everywhere else. I've learned to enjoy the peace here. That is priceless for me.

Another thing I've learned is respect for resourcefulness. The local people impressed me so much with how they come up with solutions for nearly anything, using whatever is on hand. It never ceases to amaze me, and I think it's made me a more creative thinker. I've also learned to do without a lot of things that I took for granted, and I have realized they are not important. I don't even miss them. Learning Spanish has expanded how I use words.

MS. What do you do here?

WR. My first two years here, I thought I was retiring and spent time painting and writing and growing my own food. I enjoyed not working. Eventually I became a bit bored because it wasn't enough to keep me stimulated. I created a niche for myself that didn't exist before, and that was overseeing construction for people who couldn't be here while their homes were being built. I was their eyes and ears. Todos Santos was experiencing a boom. I could have used a service like that. I advertised with a hard hat with flowers and sequins on it and got all the big projects. That was successful for a few years and then the economy took a downturn.

That morphed into a quarterly magazine called *Building in Baja…Solid Advice from the Trenches*. The focus was to help people avoid mistakes and provide practical advice when building a life, home, or business here. It covered lots of topics from design to growing food to spotlight interviews with people who were doing things in Todos Santos. It morphed again into a digital newsletter called *Baja Tips Weekly…Solid Tips with a Twist*. It grew to include four thousand six hundred subscribers worldwide. It was a lot of work, but I kept it up.

MS. I remember that one. You had so many wonderful articles on such a wide range of topics. I was impressed by the time it took you to research each issue.

WR. After three years, I realized I was overworking and needed to slow down again. My appendix burst, and I nearly died. While recovering, I was forced to rethink my life and the way I was living it. I decided to spend more time relaxing and enjoying why I chose to come here in the first place! Being me, that didn't last long. My new venture was to open a clothing boutique with my own label, Drool. I designed all the pieces and had them made locally. Within a year, I knew that the retail business was not for me.

For three years, I also wrote an anonymous column in *EL Calendario*, now called *Journal del Pacifico*. It was called "Encounters of an Underground Milkmaid." I and an interpreter interviewed only people who were born and raised here. We spent many an afternoon speaking to some very interesting characters about their lives and history here. Not only did I learn so much about the town and its people, but I made many friends that way.

It served as my integration into the Mexican culture. I got an intimate glimpse into how people live here—some with dirt floors yet a lot of pride and generosity. They accepted me, and I made minicelebrities out of them. In 2007, I turned those columns into a book—*Genuine People of Interest, Todos Santos* which is still selling at "Tecolote Book Store" and the Hotel California. It's also available digitally through my website, wendyrains.com. It's become a classic, since it captures a very distinct time in this town's history before the big boom and some of the people are no longer with us. I donated a part of the profits from the sale of the book to Cam Ten, the special-needs school here. There are a lot of kids with problems because there were only five families in this town to begin with, so it is hard not to marry your cousin.

Wendy also had one of the only English radio shows for three years on Cabo Mil. The first one was called *Todos Santos Today*. Then it changed airtime and became *Todos Santos Tonight*, and for the past year, it aired on Saturday afternoons as *Weekends with Wendy*. Wendy explained what a huge amount of work it demanded of her, since she recorded everything remotely, not like the hosts in Cabo who sit in the studio and go home after their show. Besides all the prep time for her interviews, she also had to learn how to record, edit, add music and tracks, and so on in order to send a completed program to the station. She also wrote and recorded many of the ads for her advertisers. As she said, "It was very stimulating for me, but way too time-consuming for very little return."

Wendy then launched into another aspect of herself that I have noticed in my time here: environmental activism.

WR. I was a professional activist in the States—a grassroots lobbyist on behalf of water and wetland issues in Washington, DC, and Sacramento. The struggle for the wetlands in LA brought me to write a chapter in a book for Harvard University called "Facilitating Watershed Management." Of course, I burned out—my comrades called my high salary "combat pay"—and that's why I'm here.

But when the dunes started to be sold off, I couldn't sit back and watch that happen. Nowhere in the world is that allowed to happen; they are there for a reason: protection! A group was formed to stop it. Talk about lessons learned. I've learned about corruption, deceit, greedy developers who think they are above the law, and the extent of nastiness people will go to when they feel threatened by those who want to preserve and protect habitats, whether turtle-nesting sites, palm groves, aquifers, lagoons, pristine mountains, or shorelines.

It takes money to fight back. And a very thick skin. I have learned how not to feel the victim because I've been targeted, how strong I am, how my integrity is solidly in place, as well as how willing I am to take a stand for doing what is right on behalf of future generations. I have learned how much I love and care about this place I have chosen as my home.

MS. I remember those times. You are very courageous.

WR. I didn't know that about myself. I just do what I see needs doing. My friends in the States thought that I was courageous to move here and drive Baja Highway One, which I've done twenty-nine times.

MS. Besides the continuing environmental defense challenges, what other challenges have you encountered here?

WR. Every day here presents challenges. You don't even have to leave home. Every single thing has a short life-span, especially those items dependent on power. Whether it's a washing machine, telephone, pump, TV, irrigation system, front gate, hot-water heater, fountain, pool equipment—you name it; it will die when you need it most, even if it isn't old. I have to be prepared for unexpected and unforeseen breakdowns every day and take them in stride. Always there is irregular water service, power outages, wilted lettuce, new batteries that are dead, unopened milk that is bad because the power went out at the store and they sold it anyway.

But probably the biggest challenge is keeping my sense of humor. I do my best to find the humor around me all the time. If you can't live with the outrageous excuses, tape being used to patch anything that breaks, rusting metal furniture, swollen and shrinking wooden doors and window frames, geckos and other odd creatures sharing your home, you don't belong here. Oh, yeah, dating is a *huge* challenge! There's a lack of decent single men here.

MS. And what about the future?

WR. The design business has really picked up with some large projects in Loreto Bay, which is buzzing with infusions from wealthy investors. I'm in a position now to choose what I want to do. I will continue the good fight to defend the environment. Our numbers have grown substantially, and we are affecting enforcement of legislation and making a difference. So no giving up on that front, especially since there will always be a need for soldiers in those battles. I can only hope that we will inspire the youth in our community to continue to treasure our resources and become caring stewards of this magical oasis.

MS. You have optimism and confidence that justice can win in favor of the good of all. You are a valuable citizen of our town.

WR. Thank you so much, Moonstone. You are one as well, and I believe it was you who once called me an earth warrior. I kind of like the sound of that.

CHAPTER 7

JO STEWART

I arrived at Jo's rental right on time and turned into her close-quartered, right-angled parking place and bumped into her Toyota Corolla. Not to worry. That is what bumpers are for. They aren't made of metal anymore, so they bounced off of each other.

Jo was waiting at the back gate, controlling her two dogs, Rumi and Honey.

"Stay down," she commanded with a serious-for-her tone of voice. We all made friends and then went into her rental, a five-hundred-square-foot casita with terraces out in the sun and shade—outdoor living being the big thing in such a nice climate as Baja California Sur, Mexico. She paid $400 a month plus gas, electric, and Wi-Fi connection.

We sat at the table and went right to it. Jo was seventy years young and came to this little town at the end of the peninsula four years ago from Little Rock, Arkansas. She had a master's degree in journalism and taught for many years at all levels of education from Head Start to college freshman-level English.

It was on-again, off-again, as the workload included so much extra time reading papers and discipline problems with uninter-ested students. She used her skills later while living in Mexico by being an editor for students in foreign lands writing their papers in English, not their first language. It was supplementary income, but now she was not doing it, choosing instead to read more for her own enjoyment. She was an avid reader and belonged to a book club here, where other lovers of the word shared reading the same book or similar books on a related theme, such as Mexican life and history. Jo was very relaxed and happy, with a round face with lots of smile lines and bright blue eyes.

MS. What brought you to Mexico?

Jo Stewart (JS). My brother had a time-share in Cancun, but we started coming to Cabo for a week at a time because it was closer to where he lived. We would drive up to Todos Santos for a visit. I liked it.

MS. What motivated you to stay in Mexico?

JS. I had wanted to live outside the United States for years. But I had trouble with my knees and was unable to travel. I had operations on my knees and then got on social security, which gave me a new lease on life. I felt free and competent to make a bold move like that. I took the editing job to boost my transitional income and worked in the early hours online with students all over the world.

MS. Where did you live when you first arrived?

JS. I found a house-sit for six months on a busy, dusty street in the district called *El Otro Lado* [the other side] in Todos Santos. I was really in love with Todos Santos and went back to Little Rock and put my house on the market. It sold in four months at a loss. Packing the car with everything I could get in it and on a top rack, I drove out the driveway, feeling a weight lifted from my shoulders. Of course my family and brother were worried and full of doubt. I was a little, too, about driving so long a distance into Mexico by myself. But I was also excited. I really wanted to do it.

At this time, Jo's face was a lit-up, full moon of glee and every laugh line smiling. Seeing her grin, I could picture the smile then and knew her feeling as she had driven away from the past into a future she always wanted for herself. I had done the same thing.

Jo said, "I made it to where I wanted to be!"

In fact Jo was so smiley and attractive that she was chosen for a fashion-show model last winter in the open-air French restaurant in Todos Santos. A dress shop in Cabo San Lucas and a jewelry designer put on a promotional show to a large crowd of mostly gringas. "You, too, can look as beautiful as these fabulous ex-pats in these upbeat, flowing clothes!" was the message sent by using nontraditional models, real people. Fun!

MS. No doubt you like it here, but why?

JS. The beauty of it! I have never lived in a desert environment before. It's sunny in the winter. I was one of those people who could get depressed in the winter gloom. There are interesting things to do, and I love the women who live here. I find it easy to relate to people. Now after four years, I want to expand my close friendships. I am an introvert, and I'm now reaching out after the initial surge of knowing a lot of people but not so intimately.

MS. Knowing that transitions can be difficult, what have been some of your challenges, the not-so-comfortable-parts of the move?

JS. Well, the Mexican bureaucracy is a pain to work with. To avoid it, I continue to go back to the States every six months for a visit and then renew my visitor's six-month visa upon reentry. Not knowing the language is difficult. I have taken a years' worth of lessons, and today I made an appointment on the phone. That was difficult, but I practiced it before I called. Off and on, I have taken online Spanish, but it's so intense trying to listen and comprehend Spanish. I get tired trying. There is also the frustration of not finding what you want when you go shopping. I've learned to wait for friends to bring things down or to do without. Maybe I really didn't need it. Another bit of advice for the shopper here: When you see something, get it then, because it may never be restocked. You may not find it again! I observe and laugh at myself.

Jo's frustrations were very familiar to me. I knew all these frustrations really well myself.

"And the dust!" we both said at the same time.

"So why did you stay?" I asked.

Jo said, "When I lived in the States, I was a news junkie. I kept up with all the details. I got angry with the US government: the greed, the wars, the ignorance. I just don't want to deal with it anymore. It upset me so much. Living in Mexico is an escape; it is more relaxing for me. Of course Mexican politics are awful, but there is a certain distance between me and them because I'm a foreigner."

Jo was quite active in her former US life. She worked for nonprofits, helping to start a woman's shelter and farmer's market. Now her involvements included efforts to stop an open-pit, cyanide-leach gold mine at the top of the watershed in the Sierras east of Todos Santos. Also, she helps out the residential facility [*el internado*] which houses rancho kids who spend all week in town in school and return to the ranchos on weekends.

MS. "Do you ever think of buying here?"

JS. Not really. I don't have the money for that. But I am astounded at how cheaply I can live here. It's affordable, and owning would mean a lot of maintenance and added expense.

MS. How do you spend your time?

Jo's shoulder-length, blond-brown page boy swung around as she considered the question. The effect was a halo framing a joyful face.

JS. Watch TV and movies, read, and go to dinner with friends. Every morning I take the dogs to the beach a half mile away and walk with them. I used to dance more, but not so much now. Every third year Thanksgiving is on my birthday, so a few years ago, I threw a big party at a restaurant with a lot of space for dancing. The food was fantastic! I'm involved with local issues and enjoy my type-A friend, who has many fingers in many pies. Sometimes

I wonder if I'm getting lazy, and I think I should be doing something. I add a few plants to the garden every so often.

MS. What about a love life? Any action? [*I am always curious as to the follow-ups on the flirtations of Mexican men. Seems to be a part of the culture.*] Have you integrated into the Mexican culture?

JS. Well, flirting, yes. Had one horrible experience, and then one went nowhere...both with Mexican men. I wouldn't mind meeting someone, but it is definitely not a big deal. There aren't that many great men here: married, losers, drunks, criminals. I have good relations with the people who work for me, but then I don't see them that often. For a small town, I am surprised how seldom I see folks.

MS. Is this home then? Do you think of moving on?

JS. Well, where would I go? Not the United States; I can't afford it. I enjoy it here; I'm relaxed. Everything is so fast in the United States, and you are always in a car! Of course after the direct-hit hurricane last fall, I considered leaving, but to where is a good question.

MS. What of the future?

JS. Now I am fairly healthy and will worry about it when I have to decide if something comes up.

Jo and I agreed to have dinner together on Saturday because, I, too, wanted to get to know better the people I'd been smiling at and bumping into at art openings and social events for the fourteen years I had been here. We met at a long *palapa*-roofed restaurant with a packed dirt floor. The restaurant roasted pork on a vertical spike before a flame, called La Pastor, or pulled pork. Tasty. Casual, not expensive, and, like most places here, without walls. A breeze, a view. Life in a warm climate.

CHAPTER 8

CAROL HAMPTON

Carol Hampton was very relaxed at seventy-one, with a soft, round face and blue eyes. She lived in a very *tranquilo* [peaceful] place, just a five-minute walk to the shoreline. There were houses in sight, but they were hardly ever lived in because snowbirds come and go. One left her with a beautiful yard-art dream catcher strung with beach driftwood, shells, glass, and seaweed, which were fastened to a sturdy pole that could take the sea breezes. The snowbird would probably dig it up and take it back to his trailer compound when he returned. It was a security measure to have it in her yard in his absence. The house in front of hers was a spec house that had never sold. There was a surf camp down the way and a trailer with a caretaker parked next to the house above hers.

I was curious if she had always chosen tranquilo places to live. She offered directly, "Oh, no. I've lived in cities when I was young. I ran away from home at seventeen to become a bohemian artist in San Francisco." Carol's voice was soft though definitely sure when she answered. Carol was dressed in a comfortable T-shirt and shorts and was stretched out on the chaise longue by the sliding glass door, which was one-quarter open, allowing a cooling breeze in. She had already thought about where she wanted to be interviewed…in the chaise lounge.

I commented, "This looks like a therapy session."

She replied, "Well, talking about your life is sort of therapy."

Carol's house was two-stories, about two thousand square feet. She lived her life mostly on the second floor, where the view of the ocean and the refreshing breeze could keep nature's rhythms coming into her sitting room, home to a big table/computer desk and comfortable seating. At this level also was the bedroom and bath, a kitchen and a big, inviting deck to the south. We settled in with spicy tea and cookies and began with the first question: How did you get to Baja Sur in the first place?

Carol Hampton (CH) My husband Ed always loved Mexico and fishing. He had been to Los Barilles [*a town on the Sea of Cortez*] before we met. In my early thirties, I hitchhiked to the border in Texas and traveled by bus deep into Mexico by myself to Mexico City, Acapulco, Puerto Escondido, and Oaxaca. Ed and I met when he was forty-three and I was forty-two. We had both been married before. I had married twice in my twenties and had my son, Austin. Third time was a charm. He was funny; he made me laugh and was great to be around. I really treasure the eleven years we had together. He passed away in 1998 in Cabo San Lucas, at the tip of the peninsula.

At first we went to mainland Mexico, to a little place north of Puerto Vallarta called Rincon de Guayabitos. We were thinking of buying the house we had been renting. I went north and drove down the Baja with my son driving two car loads of stuff. We took the ferry that then ran between Cabo and Puerto Vallarta. I was terrified because I am paranoid of being on the water at night. I'm a day sailor. The deal on the house fell through, so we went back north. For several years, we drove down to Cabo, pulling an eighteen-foot boat, camping a lot. It was a fun life.

We drove down the Baja so many times on that narrow, no-shoulder road. Once we drove from Placerville, California, to Cabo in two days!

MS. Holy moly!

CH. We didn't do that again. It is such a beautiful drive, though. I have so many good memories on that road with Ed. In 1993, we leased a lot in the El Arco Trailer Park in Cabo San Lucas, which was owned by an *ejido*. We started to build a two-story house in the back corner of the park, on a hill with a million-dollar view. We financed some of the expense of building by bringing down trailers from the States and reselling them here. We both worked on building the house, plus Mexican crews. We had sixty to seventy thousand dollars into the house.

Carol showed me a panoramic photo of the view from her art studio window. It was a breathtaking view of the rocks at land's end, the arch, the glistening Pacific.

CH. Finished in 1995, the house was Ed's last big project. It was my first real art studio to call my own, and I really got into my art. I'd been looking all my life for an art studio. As an artist, you are always looking for a place where you can work. I stayed on after Ed passed in 1998. I got to live there a total of sixteen years.

The guy running the park was not paying the ejido, so in 2005, they kicked him out and repossessed the trailer park. There were lots of trailers, and people had built houses. We didn't have to leave when they kicked the manager out. The ejido ran it and let it run down for years. They actually didn't kick people out until 2014. The leases were never honored in the end. That's how I ended up here. I bought this lot in 2006, thinking that if the park situation went down, I would at least have a place.

MS. Did the ejido offer to reimburse people for their homes they had built?

CH. No. I just considered it a complete slice of life, and I felt fortunate to have been there. Back then it wasn't so easy to buy land. We had a twenty-year lease. I didn't sell the house because I would have been passing on a problem to the new owners. I just walked away from it. The park rented the house out. But with the hurricane last September, windows broke and the roof peeled back, and they asked everyone to leave the trailer park.

MS. So you made this move and built this house by yourself?

CH. Two friends and I went in on three lots together. They are all in my name because I am a citizen, so we didn't have to get *fidecomisos* [*A fidecomiso is an annual fee a foreigner pays to a bank if the person's property is within fifty kilometers from a coastline. It is a way for Mexico to safeguard their many miles of coastline. There is a move to eliminate it, "pero, vamos a ver," but we'll see.*]

Carol laughed as she told me about the building of her house here in 2008, which turned out to be a mistake by a contractor. He was to build a house for some gringos who were not present at the time, and he built it on Carol's lot by mistake. The realtor found out, and the contractor had to build the same house again two lots behind Carol's on the originally intended lot. By magic, it seemed, Carol had a house on her lot. She had to pay him for his work and for windows and doors to make it secure, but then she didn't have enough money to totally finish it. It lacked plumbing and electrical wiring and a finishing coat on the inside. The interior walls were cement block, but she finished the outside so that it would look OK and no one would bother her about it.

MS. Did anyone try to figure out how the mistake of building on the wrong lot happened?

CH. No. There didn't seem to be any reason to apply blame and embarrass anyone. We just moved forward from there. I had an unexpected house! For a couple of years, I would come up and camp in the house and let other friends stay in it. By 2010, I was shuttling possessions from Cabo to here and moved in by Christmas 2011. I was driving that road between Cabo and here during the road widening of Highway Nineteen. It was insane to be driving it. It was a crazy drive!

MS. You certainly are easygoing. Have you always been like that?

CH. In my twenties, I got into Buddhism, so I learned acceptance of things as they are. I'm also a Cancer sign, so I go with the flow pretty much. I like philosophy and religion because, why are we here? I've listened to Robert Hall's dharma talks online, but for me, it isn't an academic thing. I'm not interested in structures. If it can make your life easier, why not adopt it as a way? We have so much to learn from each other.

MS. After all these years in Mexico, what do you think about the Mexican people?

CH. I love them. They are just wonderful people. I can't say that I know them well. I have had no success in learning Spanish. I don't have a facility for languages like some people do. Mexicans are so tight with their families. My family just scattered to the winds. I was the oldest girl. I am fourth generation Californian, growing up in Walnut Creek. My grandmother raised us, and we ran wild and free in those rolling California hills with the oak trees. My brothers were the cowboys, and I was the Indian.

When I was nine, my dad remarried to a woman who had been in the army, so she was very disciplined and ran a tight house. There went the freedom, but that's life, you know. I am so grateful for those early years of freedom. I ran away four times because I had the confidence to be free. I left home for good at seventeen. One good thing about my stepmother was that she minored in fine art at UC Berkeley and had a whole library of art books. At the impressionable age of nine to ten, I soaked up art for hours at a time, studying the paintings in the books. She gave up art, but she had the tools, easels, paints, and brushes.

MS. Did you study art?

CH. While living in the Bay Area, I studied at several junior colleges. Wherever I lived, I would take classes. While living on a houseboat in Sausalito, I had a papier-mâché-mask mail-order business. I had a representative who would go to shows and take orders, and then I would fill them. In Placerville, I was a member of an art collective called Gold Country Artists. There were twenty artists who maintained a retail space, and we would rotate display positions around the store so that no one got prime property all the time.

MS. What's your legal status in Mexico?

CH. I'm a citizen. I went to a fixer in Cabo, someone who helps you through the process. He would interview a herd of gringos at one time. In 2004 to 2005, it cost one thousand five hundred US dollars and took a few months to complete. He waived the language part. I don't have travel aspirations, so I didn't get a Mexican passport. But others did.

MS. What is your source of income?

CH. I get a social security check. I think they are taking Medicare out now, because the amount recently went down. I'm below the line for paying taxes, and I get by with little cash flow. My artistic moneymaker is in portraits. I couldn't afford to live in the United States. I couldn't even afford rent. I'd be living in a van or homeless. I don't know how much I live on here. Every five years or so, I treat myself to a trip north for ten days or so. The United States is a scary place, but I do enjoy the shopping spree.

MS. What's your passion in life?

CH. What do you think? [*A big laugh followed.*] Making art, being an artist, knowing other artists. I do portraits, but I like to paint all this beauty in the environment. This painting is from a photograph on the cover of the *Gringo Gazette*. I make art cards, too. My son brings down art-stock cards and envelopes, and I just glue Costco prints of my paintings on them and write the name of the painting on the back. I'm not selling at the market anymore, because hauling things back and forth just became too much. With high blood pressure, I can't take the stress, so it's just not worth it. I have some in the bookstore in Todos Santos, and she also sells my beach-wood wind chimes.

MS. What lessons have you learned from living in Mexico?

CH. I guess I have lost my impatience. If it isn't supposed to happen that day, it doesn't. Maybe it has lowered my expectations and heightened my gratitude for what does get done. My son started a building next door to this house. It's to be an art gallery for me and living quarters for him, and who knows what it will be in the future. The workers left two months ago, saying they would return in two weeks. *Nada.* [nothing]. It's his project, so I don't have to raise my blood pressure over it.

Carol's lifestyle by the beach south of Pescadero was rugged by some people's standards. There was no municipal water or electric, so her domestic life ran on three solar panels and one marine battery. She was really glad to have a fan at night. She had a generator for appliances that needed 110-volt power. Her fridge was propane gas. She bought water delivered in a truck and recycled her waste water onto her sparse plantings. I noticed that her bathtub was still in its cardboard box, but it was cut open at the top for use as a bucket bath, because there was no drain and no plumbing to fill it. This wasn't a new situation for her. She showed me photos of the two houseboats she had built on hulls of boats and had lived in while in Sausalito, California.

MS. How much time do you spend on the computer?

CH. I just got Wi-Fi last year. It is my one diversion. I'm a Facebookoholic. If my son doesn't see me on Facebook for a few days, he calls me to see if I'm all right.

MS. Do you have any advice for readers who might be considering a move to Mexico?

CH. If you buy, get a title check, number one. Also things work out the way they're supposed to. And if they don't, then it's a lesson. If you always approach your life with gratitude for what you do have, it's a wonderful life!

Maybe Carol was so calm and relaxed because she walked her talk. Maybe she was a version of Buddhist philosophy in action. Maybe this was what happiness looked like.

CHAPTER 9
PATY RAINES

As I walked up to Paty's casita in the RV park, I was greeted by a mermaid metal sculpture on the fence announcing, "*Mi Cueva Gitana.*" Paty called her space My Gypsy Cave. For $220 a month, she leased space and built her "cave", consisting of a dining area, daybed sofa and conversation zone, and a kitchen with a brick oven in the corner. All under a *palapa* roof, which she said later she didn't even want: "I just wanted the sunlight, but it warped the cupboard doors."

She proudly showed me her new kitchen addition of a sink and the stairs leading to a second-story terrace with ocean and mountain views. Next to this lovely outdoor living area was a casita, thirty feet by twelve feet, made of cement and finished nicely in warm tones of golden yellow. In it, she had an indoor bed, which had not been the case for the first eight months when she had slept on the daybed under the *palapa* roof. The 350-square-foot casita had a made-to-order closet and bathroom, with the "never do it again" pedestal sink—no storage. She felt that she had achieved the balance between in and outdoor living, a Baja Sur possibility that many a gringo fantasized as paradise.

Paty was seventy-four now and had the demeanor of an angel. She smiled a lot beneath a wreath of curly, gray hair, which was always held off the face by gauzy wraps, usually in earthy tones. Her sweet voice went along with her looks, soft and lovely. Who would think she had a will for adventure and confidence to carry it off?

We sat at her table and drank tea as she recalled what brought her to Baja. Paty said, "In the mid-1990s, I came with family and friends—my daughter and her two children, two grandkids, six to ten people—to a condo in Cabo San Lucas. It was big and accommodating, and we all had fun. We had use of the owner's car. Friends who lived in an RV on the beach in Los Cerritos [*the swimming and surfing beach outside of the small town of Pescadero, thirty miles up Highway 19 from the cape*] invited us to come up for a day's adventure. I fell in love with the area. In 2008, I drove my RV down with my pug dog, TaZzi, and came to this spot. I didn't speak any Spanish, but it was all OK.

MS. Any adventures or thrilling moments along the way?

Paty Raines (PR). The first time I drove down, I was traveling behind a friend in his car. The road down the peninsula is so narrow with no shoulders and then a drop off of a foot or more, usually more. A gigantic eighteen-wheeler was coming toward me, and I went off the road to avoid being hit. The RV bumped down the embankment, almost hit some concrete posts, and I gradually drove it back onto the road without ever stopping. There was some damage to the RV, but down low, not much.

MS. Wow! Quite a save! I've driven that road four times, and I can well imagine the tension of it all. How did you gain the experience to drive a big rig like that?

PR. Right before the worldwide market crash, I sold my house in Santa Cruz and rented a condo. My granddaughter who had been living with me decided to go back and live with her mother. I paid off all my debts, retired from my job, and bought an RV. At sixty-five in three weeks' time, I was free to live a dream.

Actually the dream was inspired by John Steinbeck's book *Travels with Charlie.* I drove the RV around the States and into Canada four times and would drive down to this very spot every winter.

MS. So this must have reinforced the idea of being a gypsy.

PR. With my birth family and in young adulthood, I moved a lot and was always independent. I was never afraid to go by myself somewhere. I have always made friends easily, anywhere—road stops, restaurants, garbage dumps. [*She chuckled now as she remembered the fun times of meeting new people.*] And now I love Facebook. I keep up with friends from the fourth grade. Half of my friends are family I have met on the road in the RV.

MS. How is your financial world working out in Baja?

PR. I have always worked. In Silicon Valley, I worked in marketing and publishing and was a personnel director. Then when I moved to Santa Cruz, I began a second career as the office manager of a big dental office, which lasted twenty-six years. I get almost two thousand dollars a month in social security, so after all the building is done, I'll be set to travel again. I'm hardly finished at seventy-four. I want to go to Cuba and cruise to Panama, and I'd love to go to Europe.

MS. So at some point, you must have sold the RV, because now you have a concrete casita where it was parked.

PR. Because I had parked here every winter, the owners told me back in 2010 that if I wanted to build here, I could. Yes, selling the RV is a lovely story to tell. I didn't advertise except on Facebook. Friends in Portland, Oregon, saw the post and knew their friends wanted a Mercedes-engine RV. They put me in touch with their friend, and we talked on Facebook. He and a friend flew down with a one-way ticket and drove the RV back. [*Paty was laughing, her round face shining at the good fortune of it all.*] All the money had been tied up in fixing the RV to sell. When it sold, I had some money to build.

MS. You broke your wrist a few years ago. That must have introduced you to the Mexican medical community.

PR. A friend and I walked to a restaurant close by, and I tripped on a typical Mexican hazard—a sidewalk. It was a sidewalk on top of another sidewalk held together with bolts sticking up. That's how I fell, landing on my arm. No suing in Mexico. No money for a private doctor, so I had to use Seguro Popular, which was disappointing for many reasons. But I was initially discriminated against because the doctor had an attitude about rich gringos coming to Mexico and using the national welfare insurance. So I didn't have a surgeon. I went to the La Paz hospital every day, hired an interpreter, and had to find a driver each time. I was no longer an emergency, so they put me off for two months. The surgery was not successful, because the bone had grown out to here during the two-month wait. [*She gestured about three inches from the outside of her arm.*] Now I have Sky Med, which will fly me door to door to the hospital of my choice in the States, where I have Medicare.

MS. That all sounds disappointing, but you solved the problem for future missteps. How do you spend your time down here?

PR. Since I've been here full-time, which has been four and a half years, I have been in five or six book clubs and women's clubs. We have a singles club. I used to read more, but now I am practically blind. I need to get that fixed. I lost my driver's license in California, so I can't drive there. I can't drive at night and can't read the signs, so I only drive where I know where I'm going. I drive my quad around Pescadero, trips to the store and the beach. I wait and wait sometimes to cross the highway until it is safe. My little pug has a basket to ride in, and she loves it.

Paty affectionately bent over to chin cuddle the black pug, and then she said, "I go to lots of potluck dinners with friends and go to Baja Beans [*a coffee-roaster cafe in Pescadero*] where they have a farmer's market on Sundays in the winter. So it's really social, and there is live music. I've been reading more with a Kindle app on my computer. I can adjust the font size, and also I've been listening to books on tape. Anything I can get on Amazon, I can read. I'm setting my house up to be a party house. I love dinner parties and cooking for others. I don't have the right pots and pans, so I want to get good ones. A guy is coming today at three to discuss building a table for me right here. A favorite restaurant has rustic but smooth picnic-like tables, so that guy is going to build one for me."

I love the community spirit of the people here. Buy local; support the people who live here.

MS. Anything else you like to do?

PR. I used to walk on the beach but not so often now. I have a degenerative disease that runs in my family. I'm not as bad as some of my family members. I'm not going to slow up too much. It's under the umbrella of muscular dystrophy. It wastes away your peripheral nervous system, not your central nervous system, so my mind will be all right. I fall a lot; my balance is off. [*She was chuckling again…so positive.*] I'm not going to let it stop me from traveling. I'll work it out with assistants to help push me in a wheelchair if that is what it takes. I do yoga every day of my life, starting out in bed in the morning, and I stretch at the kitchen bar.

MS. I know you from the singles group, so I know you wrote a brief autobiography this past year.

Looking humble yet pleased with herself, Paty answered, "Right after Hurricane Odile, I was inspired to write it. So without electricity, I started writing longhand. I wrote every day for two months. I was so disciplined; I wrote between three and seven hours a day. It was a cathartic experience. All people should write their story; we all have one. I found so many threads that ran through my experiences. One being I never chose men; I let men choose me. That was a big issue. I was married four times."

Paty let out a big laugh and continued, "I faced a lot of stuff. When I write the real stuff, I will write it as fiction, because I don't want to hurt anyone. Maybe I'll never publish it, but I want to leave a record for the family. We don't know each other; we never tell it all. All my older relatives are dead. I never knew them well enough. We all have a different perspective of an event."

MS. Are there challenges for you here, things that don't work for you?

PR. I suppose not knowing Spanish is a big one. I took lessons for one and a half years, and it was hard. I didn't want to spend my time studying, so I gave it up. Now that I have a TV, I want to get movies in Spanish with English subtitles. [*She gave a solid nod on that one, as if it were done.*] Then there is shopping. We often have to go to four stores to get everything on the list. And I do not like buying clothes in Mexico. I buy mine when I'm in the States. Then of course I learned that the Mexican medical system is nothing you can depend on.

MS. Do feel like you have integrated into the Mexican culture at all?

PR. Yes! The people who own the RV park are Mexican so I've been to all their children's *quinceañeras* [a sweet-fifteen party celebrating a girl's coming of age] and Christmas parties and other family events. I have good relations with the woman who cleans and the gardener. And then there is Angel, who keeps my car on the road, drives me to Cabo sometimes, installed the washing machine, and is so helpful. He never tells me what to pay him. I just appreciate him so much.

I also admire the Mexican tradition of taking care of their families. That's why there are no elder-care facilities. I love that they keep up their religious traditions. And the music they play and they sing! I hear music coming from everywhere. The men are gorgeous, too! [*She giggled.*]

Mexicans are so helpful. Once I drove my car into a hole that was not marked, and it tipped on its side. I had a hard time getting out. There were six guys helping me, and then they tipped the car back upright. One of the guys did a test drive down the highway and back to make sure it was working. I got a little concerned because my purse was there on the seat and just happened to be loaded with cash. But it was there when the car came back.

MS. How was Hurricane Odile for you and your gypsy cave?

PR. Odile was so noisy. I could hear trees crashing and the plate-glass windows across the highway hitting the ground. I spent the time in the casita breathing. I breathed my way through it. I talked to Mother Nature and became one with it, became peaceful.

MS. How much did it cost you to repair the damage?

PR. The only real damage was to the *palapa*, and it cost me about five hundred dollars to repair.

MS. What's your legal status in Mexico?

PR. I am a permanent resident. I don't want to be a citizen. I don't want to vote.

MS. Would you ever live in the United States again?

PR. Never! I don't even like to go to visit. Everything is so fast paced...and the traffic.

A rare grimace appeared on Paty's contented, cherubic face, and she shook her head for emphasis as she declared, "I'm happy here and peaceful. And I love summer!"

CHAPTER 10

KAT WILSON

In a fairy tale, Kat Wilson's house would be described as "under the hill." I parked the car and set the break on a slope, which went in two directions, and got out. Calling over the fence to the cement steps plunging down, I could see only a concrete rooftop. My call was answered by two blond dogs doing their job as doorbell.

Kat came peeping around the corner at the bottom of the steps and said, "Yes, this is the house."

It didn't look like a house from where I stood, but it was indeed a house with a magnificent view of the Pacific Ocean and the surrounding huerta. Kat gave me a quick tour of the outside: a couple of cement-slab terraces, one she hoped to set a tepee on; two sets of cement steps leading down to another level where there was a RV, used as a small guest room, parked; and a boxy, little concrete-block *bodega* [storeroom]. Also I could see a car with the hood up and guys up to their elbows in the engine compartment.

"They are buying an old car that was left here two years ago. Soon it will be gone," Kat said and smiled a wide, white smile.

The house tour continued with a view from the back porch, which was outfitted with a Mexican cot and two tables that looked like they could be worktables. I knew Kat painted tiles, so I pictured her out on this deck painting in the Pacific breeze. The view was certainly awesome, with no interruptions across the hills and houses of Pescadero, over the agricultural fields and the palms bordering them, and all the way to the blue-gray Pacific beyond.

Kat said, "I added this porch when I bought the place seven years ago. But there is too much of a breeze to really use it a lot. In the winter, the breeze is cool, so I end up inside."

This verified my observations about decks facing the ocean view: They don't get used because the winds of winter are prohibitive to lounging and eating. Before I built my house, I listened to the advice of a longtime resident, who said, "Every house should have two porches. One facing the west, the ocean, and the sunset; the other one facing the east, the mountains, and the sunrise." I did that in the house I designed for myself and have never regretted it. In my L-shaped house, the east porch sits in the angle of the *L* with the house as a windbreak from the cold winds of winter.

Kat's house consisted of two rooms with a bathroom off a small hallway, probably no more than four hundred square feet. One room for sleeping and entertaining; the other for cooking, eating, entertaining and doing small art projects. Both rooms were packed with memorabilia and stacks of books; the rooms were neat and tidy with a comfortable feeling. The kitchen had some nice furniture holding kitchen things. One whole wall was two feet deep in plastic boxes of organized raw materials for her artistic talents.

We sat at the table and commenced our interview. I asked Kat how she came to the Baja peninsula and when.

Kat said, "In July 1991, I arrived in Cabo San Jose with my Italian husband. We had just spent one and half years in Italy. I didn't like Italy because we were housed four stories up in a big city and I'm really a small-town girl from Iowa. We came to Cabo San Jose for him to chef in Da Giorgio, and I managed the dining room. We lived right there. The restaurant was only open at night, so all day I enjoyed the good life at the beach and only went into town once a week for supplies. Within a year, he was gone. We were both Geminis, so there were four people in the relationship instead of two. But I stayed in San Jose for a total of seventeen years."

MS. That's a long time. Did you work at Da Giorgio the whole time?

Kat Wilson (KW). Only for two years.

MS. But you were still living in San Jose?

KW. Yes. I house-sat in an area called Chamizal, on the east side of town. One road in, one road out, with arroyos on either side. We did a lot of walking and exploring the arroyos. I had the same house-sit every winter for eight years. I acquired another boyfriend, strangely also an artist from Iowa.

Looking at Kat now at sixty-three, I could well imagine her twenty years ago. She was tall and willowy, and the sleek, draping, rayon, black-and-white-print dress she was wearing was becoming and fitted the graceful style she chose for her life.

MS. I know you as a talented craftier and painter of tiles. How did that come about?

KW. While working at the restaurant, I met a Laguna Beach emigrant artist who turned me on to snorkeling at what used to be Punta Bella, near the old Pamilla Resort. A new love was found. The colorful magic of the underwater world captured my artist's imagination. Sometimes we would go out three times in a week. A strong creative bond was built, and we shared a booth at an art fair in Cabo Plaza Bonita in 1991. She and I made fifteen pairs of painted-leather earrings and sold a bunch. I had crafted in painted leather before when I lived in Colorado. In 1992, I painted my first tiles with a friend, Chrissy, and fired them in a kiln we rented in La Paz.

I did one of the first Todos Santos art shows at the El Molino trailer park. There was a twice-a-year craft show at Cabo Marina called SPLASH, for local artists and Mexicans alike. I also sold at the Los Barriles Art Show for over twenty years. I sold in the

La Jolla annual craft show, which was the first big waterfront re-sort in San Jose. For a few years in San Jose, there was Art in the Garden on Saturdays, which was really beautiful, right down in the plaza. There were huge trees, and the artists' kids would play in the trees.

That is where I learned to speak Spanish. The artists were from Argentina, Columbia, and other South American countries, so it wasn't just Mexican Spanish, which I had picked up managing the restaurant and being the go-between for the waiters, who knew only Spanish, and the diners, mostly gringos, and the kitchen staff. I was not legal to sell then, and they all protected me and hid me when trouble arrived.

Art shows and markets are fun, but the tiles are heavy! My South African friend, Annie, got an in at the Westin selling her superb jewelry, so she took my first tiles there to sell. It was re-ally a short season from November to April, and then she would return to the mainland when the tourist season petered out. So for ten years, I sold her jewelry and my tiles from a gift cart at the Westin. It sat down by the pool near the beach, and I could watch the whales go by in their season. During that period, Chrissy and I painted together and sold many murals of the underwater world we loved so much.

MS. So why did you want to move to Pescadero?

KW. I loved San Jose. But it started to get too big, and traffic was building up. I had a car stolen out in Chamizal, and the houses out there were always being broken into because the arroyos are walking paths. Just to get out of the arroyo onto the frontage road was frustrating because of the increase in cars going by. I couldn't live with it. I received an inheritance in 2007. Just before the bot-tom dropped out, I sold the family home in Iowa and was able to buy this house in Pescadero. I've also invested in a couple of lots here. I'd never owned land before. But the US dollar was dropping quickly, and I didn't want to just lose it all.

With that, Kat began a tale of land ownership and the way that it becomes complicated and the dream fizzles. In 2008, Kat and a girlfriend bought a lot in La Rivera on the other side of the peninsula. She paid to fence and clean it. Then last year she heard from the realtor that a corporation from Colorado owned three lots and said that her lot was theirs. Upon going there and checking things out, Kat found out that, yes, indeed it was their lot. Kat's lot was the scruffy one in front of the one she had cleaned and fenced. with eight meters of land missing at one end.

Kat said, "I would never have bought that scruffy little lot for thirty thousand dollars! Then last March I hear from a lawyer who said that my 'not lot' had been sold in 2000 to someone else. So basically the Mexican sold the lot twice. Now I am in court to get my money back. I am just waiting to hear from the lawyer, who has now changed his phone number. I would say to anyone buying property here, get a title search either through the realtor or a company that does that sort of thing. It only costs a couple hundred dollars.

MS. After all that, did you get a title search for this house?

KW. No, because the owners had a *fidecomiso*, so the bank that holds the *fidecomiso* does a title search.

MS. Did you have to buy a new *fidecomiso*, or did you just assume the one the owners had?

KW. Neither, because I am a Mexican citizen.

MS. How did that happen?

KW. Most people have to go to Mexico City twice to get it, but here a friend had a friend from Mexico City who helps gringos go through the process. He came for a visit, and I had my first interview right here. Then he met me in Mexico City, and we finished the process. What was more difficult was getting the legal papers to be an artist here. You have to have an art degree or records of galleries you have displayed in. Now that I'm a citizen, I can do whatever I want to earn money. I have to pay sales tax, but then they changed those laws two years ago and made it more difficult for us little guys.

MS. So how are you doing financially?

KW. Pretty good! I now get a small social security check, and this past winter season I worked in a friend's chocolate shop in Todos Santos. So I feel like I can live on about four to five hundred dollars per month. I have some of the inheritance left and some debts I can call up if things get tight.

MS. How's your health?

KW. Great mostly, but like many artists and musicians, as we age, we begin to suffer. I've had to ease off the tile painting, because my hands and fingers are going numb. I think some of it is the heavy use of my hands. I hold a lot of tension in my shoulders, too. Then I developed trigger thumb and fingers, where they contract and don't open up all the way, limiting my movement quite a bit. Also the kiln developed an electrical problem and has not been fixed.

The only health insurance I have is the Seguro Popular. They gave me three free years, and I have not needed to use it in the first two. Thankful for that. I kept a very expensive policy in the United States but never used it, and it wasn't worth it. I would be very grateful to end my earth walk right here. I would never go back to live in the United States. I hope some of my close friends will soon wake up and join us down here in paradise.

MS. Have you integrated with the Mexican culture?

KW. Yes, I think so. I know a lot of the language and am on a first-name basis with the people here. A lot of the local and different dialects here are difficult for me to catch. But here in Pescadero and Todos Santos, I relate more to gringos, and I feel I'm losing some of my language skills.

MS. You stayed in Mexico because you like it?

KW. I love it. Because of the freedom and the natural beauty of Baja.

MS. Describe "freedom."

KW. I used to go visit my mom, and first, the cat has to be on a leash. Then the cat has to be registered. It's changed a lot in the past twenty-four years. It's not the home of the free anymore. Here I have rarely had to show any papers to anyone. I love Baja because of its natural beauty. As an artist, it is so hauntingly beautiful, still a bit wild and open. I am between the incredible Pacific sunsets and the mountains behind me, with the awesome dense desert all around. I am surrounded by the grace of Mother Nature, and I pray that we can learn to protect and nurture this great land and not continue to exploit it for greed and corruption.

MS. What about challenges?

KW. You mean the proposed gold mine at the top of the water shed or the drug-cartel movements? In the beginning, there were a lot of different challenges. No one had cell phones or home phones, no Costco. I'm challenged by the mistreatment of the animals; it's hard to see. And then finally realizing you can't save them all. Save one, and there are two more the next day. The garbage litter is bad. And the abuse of women, when you become aware of it, is pretty bad. Baja has the highest rate of unwed pregnancies in all of Mexico.

For fifteen years. I was a part of a charity in San Jose called LEGAMAC. It's a foundation that raises money to help Mexicans. It started out helping the old people who were falling through the cracks because there is no social security here, but it has had many projects, including buying school uniforms for the children. Uniforms cost about one hundred dollars. We were able to supply close to four hundred kids with uniforms, plus backpacks and school supplies. It seems that wherever gringos have gone in Mexico, they have been big donors in efforts to help. Mostly we are retired, so we're not taking anything from the system but adding to it and trying to help the needy animals and unfortunate people who we're able to reach in spite of our differences. Love opens doors.

MS. What are some of the Mexican traits that have impressed you?

KW. They are very generous, friendly, and warm. They put family first. It's a country of heart, not so much greed. I have never had a need on the highway that a Mexican hasn't stopped to help. Oh, yeah, I love the siesta tradition. Of course there are petty crimes, but not until last year were there any violent crimes. I have felt victimized by robbery; my car has been vandalized with rocks through the windows twice when the neighbors had a party. Now I have put mirrors around my property facing out, hoping to send negative energy back out. It's been OK since then. Of course I drive defensively. They're not the greatest drivers; often there is no testing of laws or skills here. My dog was poisoned but lived. I've been here long enough to see changes, like the young people are ruder, less courteous than they used to be, but that is true in other places, too.

MS. Have you ever been frightened?

KW. Sometimes when the dogs bark for a long time at night. It was sad after the big hurricane last September when two drug cartels started eliminating each other. Right down the street, there was a rat-a-tat-tat of gunfire, and it sounded like it was on my back porch. The hurricane was pretty frightening. The door blew open, and after getting it closed, I spent the rest of the night praying that the buckling door stayed closed. My bathroom window blew out, so I had some flooding in there and glass on the floor. But I didn't suffer too much damage. I was praying on my knees, giving thanks when I got the door shut. I chanted, "*Om Mani Padme Hum*," to Kwan Yin, [*the mantra of compassion and Kwan Yin is the goddess of compassionate listening*] in addition to having about seven Guadalupes around the room. I really covered all the bases of divine help. I can laugh about it now.

MS. And yet you stay.

KW. I feel grateful to live here. I feel guilty when I talk to my friends in the States. Everyone is so stressed and spends so much time in traffic.

MS. What do you do with your time?

KW. I read a lot. [*True. There were piles books stacked around the room*] I water the plants by hand. I'm a hermit, really. I don't spend a lot of time on the computer, and I don't watch many movies. I joined Facebook, so I keep up better.

MS. Do you ever get lonely or bored?

KW. Bored? Yes. It's got a bit the same, day after day, week after week, month after month. I don't have much family or children, but I do have some anniversaries of the heart when friends and loved ones have passed on. I do get lonely. I'm so thankful for my animals. I'm not really looking for a man to complete me, but there is a part of me that thinks I'm too young never to be touched again. I'm quite content living alone.

Kat seemed like she would be happy in any small town where she could do her art and make the money it took to live comfortably and simply. Her advice was buyer beware! Get a title check!

Kat's big, brown eyes looked directly into mine as she said, "I try to trust and love everyone and hope it comes back."

CHAPTER 11

LEIRION

I had been to Leirion's house on the hill above Los Cerritos Beach a couple of times before, but it had been years ago, when she and a friend had been hosting meditation circles for interested souls in process. I was following recent directions but still had my doubts that I had turned at the right dirt road, so I backtracked, decided I had been right, and headed further up the hill looking for Two Can Road. I found it, but I was late. Leirion didn't seem to mind. Her soft demeanor welcomed me with a hug, and she asked what she could have added to the directions to make it clearer. A humble woman indeed.

I loved Leirion's little, round, one-room house when I had come before, and I was looking forward to this interview not only because it was with a woman whom so many people admired and spoke well of but also because I would get to be in her life-size hobbit house. It reminded me of my back-to-the-land years when we built earth lodges in the round to make it through the northern winters. It must have had good fêng shui, because it was relaxing in its embrace and yet expanding in the overall view of the beach and the expanse of the Pacific below.

The walls were made from woven *palo d'arco* sticks that had been stuccoed on the inside to make a flat, earthen-colored wall. This is a time-honored building style in southern Baja, because very few nails are required. *Palo d'arco* trees are plentiful and have the characteristic growth pattern of coppicing, which means that when they are cut six or more inches above the root, they produce more shoots, which will grow quickly into another stick to cut. *Palo d'arco* is mostly used for its long, thin sticks. If cut on the full moon, it has a resistance to bug infestation. It is used as the building material for so many things in Baja: fences, gates, walls, furniture, *barra* [crossbars] in the *palapa* roofs, *media sombra* [medium shade, sometimes called a ramada locally], trellises, firewood, and so on. It is one of those valuable gifts from nature not overlooked by the original inhabitants.

The roof was *palapa*-style, made from the palm fronds of the Washingtonian palm tree endemic to Baja Sur. The Washingtonian palm is very drought and fire-resistant in this harsh climate of few rainfalls. It can live on and on when other trees die. Its fronds have many purposes, and the tree produces new ones many times after the dead ones have been harvested for *palapas* or fencing.

On the beach side of her house was a semicircular *palapa* roof over a patio with table, chairs, and hammock. What a honey of a house to spend your days in! There was a kitchen counter set as an island with enough space behind it for storage. The bathroom was a composting style, outside a short walk away, with a shower attached.

I was so happy just sitting there and setting up the microphone that I forgot the interview and blurted out how much I loved her house.

Leirion offered, "I built it with a one-time inheritance from my mother. The *palapa* roof was in place. My camper trailer was parked under it for years, and I lived in the shade of the *palapa* on a dirt floor. In 2009, I built the house by simply dropping walls or building them up with the *palo d'arco*. I later replaced the dirt with a brick floor, because it was easier with the dogs I lived with. I used to have six. Now only three."

Curious about people's name when they aren't common, I started the interview with the obvious question: Is Leiron a given name or a chosen one?

Leirion (L). Leirion is my birth name. I let go of my last name after my divorce. That was before the age of computers, and I didn't realize they weren't prepared to accept one name. Especially down here, where the custom is for the mother and father's last names to be on the document, it requires lots of wordy explanations. My American passport has only "Leirion"; my Mexican passport has my mother and father's name on it. But my Mexican citizenship has only one name.

Ten years ago, I became a citizen and have been here at Cerritos Beach twenty-seven years. At first I camped in the Airstream on the beach. I had a dream of a tidal wave here. So I went to the ejido office and asked if I could camp further up the hill on higher ground. Yes, I could, for one hundred US dollars a year. Then when they sectioned off the land, I bought the land I was camped on—three lots, or six thousand square meters. There is the trailer still parked up here beside the house. My son came and helped me with all that. I have six children.

MS. How old are you, Leirion?

L. Eighty-three. When I turned seventy, it felt like the hard part was over. I was fifty-six when I came here. I was married for twenty-seven years. The children were all out of the house except two in high school. This was in New Hampshire, and I thought I would live the rest of my life there. The house had been in my family, so when we divorced, I got it. It was the house with my heart. Built in 1780, post and beam, on eighty acres. Hand hewn, no nails, all from trees on the land. That is why I like this little house; it is hand built.

I had been in Jungian therapy as a patient and then became a therapist. On that path, I came to know on a gut level that our purpose in life was to have union with our higher self…the moksha. From Jungian psychology, I realized that was the goal. So I wanted a teacher who had done that, had accomplished that, because I didn't think I could do it by myself. I made the decision to find a teacher, and it was a free fall after that and still is. After I sold the farm, I found Sai Baba.

MS. Is Sai Baba a Hindu, a universal person? A historical person or living?

L. He is no longer living. I'll show you a picture. [*She went to get a picture of a smiling guy with a gnome like face and a fuzzy, black Afro.*] Once I made the decision to find a teacher, it was like I took the bait and was reeled in. I didn't know where I was going, but I headed southwest. I had a dream, which showed me arriving at a city on a high plateau ringed by mountains. Coming through passes in the mountains were thousands who, like me, had all given up everything in answer a call from God. I met someone who knew Sai Baba, a master who said our purpose as humans was to attain Adviata, or divine union with the higher self. I thought this could be my teacher. Before I knew it, I was on the next plane to India. That whole process took about two years.

MS. Nothing so amazing as intention bearing fruit. How was India?

L. I spent three months in an ashram checking him out, to see if he really was God incarnate in a human form—or universal consciousness, if you don't want to use religious terms. I tested him in every way I could think of because I'm such a skeptic.

MS. Tell me one of the ways you tested him.

L. Oh, I have so many stories. Here's one. Sai Baba had an elephant. When I went to see the elephant, he came right over to me, and we had eye contact. I felt that Sai Baba was looking at me and that I was looking at Sai Baba through the elephant's eye. It was a global experience. Being a skeptic, I just observed that.

In the next gathering, darshan, the women are on one side and the men on the other. Sai Baba comes out and walks around. There were probably a thousand of us there. I was right up front, which happens rarely. Sai Baba came out of the temple maybe fifty feet away, walked over to me, and looked into my eyes. It was so powerful I fell over backward. Everyone around me was responding to what happened to me. It was a confirmation of the eye contact. In three months' time, there were so many confirmations.

Oh, I have to tell you this one, because it was the first one. It was Christmas, and I have always loved deeply the form of Jesus. As a child, I used to feel that presence so strongly. I was in my room grieving because it was the first time I had been away from my children at Christmastime, and I was missing the Christmas pageantry and tradition. The Christians at the ashram had formed a choir so that they could sing carols. I joined it, and now was the time for a rehearsal. So I told myself, no matter how sad I am, get going! At the place where we met, there was a small altar with candles and usually a picture of Sai Baba, but the picture was of another man who I felt sure was Jesus. The woman next to me said, "Yes, it is Jesus."

"But it can't be," I said. "It's a photograph."

"Well, go ask that man. He took the picture."

I asked him, "Who is that?"

He said, "It's Jesus. I took a photo of Sai Baba, and when I developed it, that is what came out."

I took the photo to Sai Baba and asked him who it was.

Sai Baba said, "That is Jesus three days before he died."

I have seen many paintings of Jesus but never one like this: a Jewish man, very ascetic looking, with a very high forehead and with the piercing eyes of a realized being. I came away knowing that he was who he said he was and that he was my guru. When my three-month visa was up, I returned to the States.

I had so many fears that I know that I could not have come this far all by myself, leaving my home and family, without this deep connection to Sai Baba. The time at the ashram was a time of internalizing that presence. Sai Baba personifies for me the higher self, someone I could dialogue with, take my fears to, and say, "I'm at a loss. What am I going to do now?" I ask my higher self all kinds of practical things.

Adviata is a process of union with the higher self. Through my Jungian work, I knew there was something that knew me perfectly and wanted the highest good for me always. I asked Sai Baba, "Why do I need you when I have dealt with that before?" He said, "It is like a child and parent: you see it; then you internalize it; then you are it, a parent. You see the light; you are in the light; then you are the light."

It made it a lot easier for me to have an outer guru. I don't think it is any different than people who honor the Buddha until they realize that they are that. Or Christians who honor Jesus and then realize they are an incarnation of Christ's consciousness. No different.

MS. So now do you just live life with your higher self and know the answers from that part of you who can see the present, the past, and the future? Or do you reach these points where you don't know what to do next?

L. I think that is why a material guru helps. Sometimes I think I have always been challenged by the material world. Getting a car serviced and all things I relied on my husband for. Sometimes I say, "OK, Sai Baba, you're my husband now; what am I going to do about this mess?" And synchronicity will happen. There was a lot of fear at first, even with Baba.

MS. It's hard to face this big world alone at fifty-six, fifty-seven. Maybe too late.

L. Carl Jung would say it is absolutely the right moment, because that is when individuation happens.

MS. What brought you to Baja Sur?

L. I had asked Sai Baba, "Where should I go, the United States or Mexico?" He said, "Mexico, because the United States is too expensive." I had been living on the money from selling my land. Sai Baba said, "Invest the money, and live on the interest. Keep it for yourself."

I thought he was going to say, "Give it to the poor." I needed to hear that, because I was one to always give things away. I still have the interest from the sale of the land and farm, plus my husband's social security. All this was on faith. If I'd thought about it, I wouldn't have done it. I do know from my work as a therapist that when you take the first step, the way opens.

MS. What was that like to be camping out on the beach with your trailer?

L. I drove down the Baja, not knowing where I was going to land. In Los Barriles, I lost my cat, so I stayed until I found her. Someone there told me it was getting expensive in Los Barriles and that she knew Mary Lou Stewart in Todos Santos, who had rooms to rent. We had dinner in Todos Santos, and I saw the procession for La Dia de Guadalupe. I said, "Oh, I have to be here for Christmas." I never left.

I tried to leave to find better swimming beaches, but every time, one of my children would call and say they were coming to visit. One son spent all summer. By that time, I had made connections and was comfortable dry camping, without hookups for my trailer. In the past, the family had done canoe camping and hiking. I called my trailer "my womb with a view." A friend's husband was a lifeguard, so for a full year, he instructed us on how to face up to those big waves. Every morning at eight, we would be there, swimming out, getting into trouble, and then getting a lesson in what we could have done differently. I eventually got comfortable, but I always wore fins. I still swim.

MS. Does your family come down to visit?

L. One child comes regularly, and the others come as they can. This Christmas a son and his three kids will come. I'll sleep in the trailer, and they'll have the house. At the end of December, four grandchildren are coming.

MS. Do they feel resentful that you left the family?

L. No. The biggest upset was selling the farm. It was harder than leaving my husband. It still is. It's still with me. For five years, I grieved that loss; then I had a dream. I was in that kitchen talking with a friend, and I said, "Why am I always back here?" The voice of Jesus said, "The love you gave here, the love you received, is who you are." The grief stopped overnight. When what we have loved becomes a part of us, there is no such thing as loss. Our environments become us, because they nurture us.

MS. I like that idea. How was Hurricane Odile for you up on this hillside?

L. I'm a part of the WWHD club: women who hold doors. I held that door closed for two and a half hours. [*She gestured to a side door.*] You can still see where my hand took the paint off the door. I learned to switch hands and feet while saying a mantra the whole time. I had no fear of hurricanes before that. I had been lying on the bed, watching the roof go up and down like an umbrella. I got frightened, and just then the door blew open. There was no room for fear then because I was too busy. The lock had been ripped off. I had my butt on the door, my hands on the wall ahead of me, my feet in the middle. I was a tripod, a very strong structure. There was a feeling of rootedness, not just one hand against the door doing it. I didn't choose to do a mantra; it just happened.

MS. The house looks good. It took the storm well. Did it cost you much in repairs?

L. This is a new thatch. [*She pointed at the beautiful* palapa *roof.*] The house insurance paid for a new roof.

MS. Wow! Insurance on a *palapa*! That is the first time anyone has ever mentioned house insurance.

L. From photos, they saw it was a house, not just an open-air *palapa*. It was a Mexican company in La Paz. They have been so good to me. I also bought car insurance from them. The house premiums are five hundred dollars a year. I knew I wouldn't be able to replace the house, so I got the insurance. During Odile, I lost the roof over the trailer, and the shower was damaged. My children contributed money also. The trailer, tied down with two cables into deep cement, was secure. Now I have it fastened with four cables.

MS. What about other challenges of being here?

L. Just learning to survive without infrastructure in the desert was a challenge. I now have solar panels and four deep-cell batteries. There are three large tanks, called *tenacos* for water storage, and the water truck fills them. The stove and fridge are propane. I have a big propane gas tank in place, and the truck fills it once a year. I didn't have a big plan; it was *poco a poco* [little by little]. Spacing out the cost, as need arose, I did it. I get a little more infrastructure each year.

MS. Do you speak Spanish?

L. Yes, I learned when I came here. I took a year of classes. I've enjoyed learning the language as I go. I'm still learning with everyone I speak with.

MS. Do you feel you have integrated into the Mexican culture?

L. To a degree. In my sixties, I had a Mexican man friend. His family took me in. They are still friendly. The day after Odile, the Mexican people who work here—the man who built it, the woman who cleans, and the gardener—turned themselves inside out to help me.

MS. What have you learned from your experience here?

L. I have learned to trust in the present and the presence. Another biggie was learning to love myself. By living by myself instead of with a family, I can feel what I am feeling. I don't think I could have learned it the same way if I were with my children and grandchildren. I needed to take a risk, go through fear, and discover that I would be supported. Any kind of growth, spiritual or physical, has an element of risk in it.

If a category-five hurricane comes, this place will go. If it comes, I've made arrangements to go to a friend's house, which is cement and rebar. There have been so many fears. I was afraid of coming down here. I have a lot of existential fears. The biggest is not being true to myself. I had to hit bottom before I could learn to listen. If you don't listen, you lose life. After Odile, I had a million questions: Do I stay? Go back to the States? Move into town? The big question is to know what the self wants. To allow all those balls in the air, to not grab at what seems safe, but to wait for clarity.

MS. You seem to have so much integrity.

L. It's been a long process. There was a time when I didn't want to be on earth at all. At this phase, being eighty-three, how much longer will I live? And what will my capacities be? I am not so fearful as before, because I have learned to trust. I was willing to change and take risks. Answers come as you go.

MS, In the many years you have been here, have you had boyfriends?

L, I know for sure I don't want a Mexican boyfriend. I had a very passionate affair with a gringo who was older than I am. Great sex, actually! Than the passion cooled on my part, and he got angry and withdrew. It was a dominating-male scenario. Another opportunity to practice what I've already learned.

MS, What do you do with your time?

L, I retired at seventy, but counseling work still comes. I feel I can see the higher self of people who come to me for help, so I can be an advocate for that voice. I can see where future growth is and encourage them in their choices. I also teach a small tarot class and do tarot readings. I swim three or four times a week and walk the dogs twice a day. The computer is a great gift, which I try to limit to an hour in the morning. Just this year I got a Kindle, so I enjoy reading a mix of fiction and nonfiction. The Palapa Society library is a good source of my reading material. I spend time with close friends, and at least once a week, I have lunch with someone. I meditate every day. Learning never ends.

MS. Your life's choices and experiences are inspirational, Leirion. Thank you so much for sharing with others on the brink of decision-making. Stepping into the unknown can feel like the fool in the tarot, stepping off the cliff with a rose in your hand and a smile on your face. Innocence and trust help us take steps away from what we know and take tentative steps on new ground. Congratulations on a successful journey!

CHAPTER 12
ZANDRA FRAME

While trying to find Zandra's house on a road I seldom drove, I passed a gray solid wall with a burnished metal Z on it. I wondered if that could be it, but I went further. Then I called, and yes, that had been it. I pulled into a shaded car park next to her car and struggled with the gate latch until a voice from above instructed me how it worked. I passed by the ground-floor house, a rectangular, gray building with nothing superfluous, just two awnings shading two doors. To the right was a landscape of desert soils and sand, dotted with desert agaves and hardy palms. Climbing the stairs to her upstairs apartment revealed that the house was situated right behind the dunes, and beyond was the endless Pacific Ocean. Turning left at the top of the stairs, I was on an open, long, wide terrace with sliding glass doors to an interior.

Zandra described herself as a modern minimalist, and she had chosen black, white, and gray as her color scheme. She told me her nickname was Zebra and that her friends called her Z. She said, "Black and white are my favorite colors, which are no colors. I always wear these colors. I've worn black my whole life." Today she was wearing all white—slim pants and stylish, loose top with a sewn diagonal pattern.

Her furniture was shaped for an easy eye with nice textures in the fabrics and indigenous weavings accenting the curves and inviting cushions. There was plenty of artwork with color on the walls and a small, round glass table with two chairs. After a quick view of the rest of the apartment (minimal kitchen, two cabinet walls facing each other for storage, and a minimal bathroom), we get down to the interview, because, true to form, Zandra had another appointment right after our time.

MS. So how did you find this tiny oasis town at the tip of the Baja peninsula?

Zandra Frame (ZF). I came with friends on a day-trip from Cabo San Lucas in 1990 and sort of fell in love with the place. Ten years later some friends had some property for sale here, and I returned for a visit. I had been coming to Mexico since I was a kid, sometimes for a week or a month—to Mexico City, Oaxaca, the Mayan peninsula, and Central and South America. I always thought I could be comfortable living in Mexico. But I never really considered living full-time and was in the market for buying a small house, not to start from scratch and build. Then eight years ago I decided to live full-time south of the border.

MS. Why did you come here?

ZF. I was looking for a permanent getaway rather than a vacation spot. I was looking for someplace close enough to easily get back to the Bay Area in northern California. In the early 1980s, I had friends coming and going from the east cape. When I first came in 1990, their place was a very cool, very rustic *palapa*, sort of like a little resort. I've always liked Mexico, and I like the warmth. I have no permanent residence up north anymore.

MS. At first did you consider coming and going every year?

ZF. I never considered not working. I was into real-estate development and historical rehab, adaptive reuse of historic buildings. It's only a two- and one-half-hour plane flight from San Francisco. Back then it was ninety-nine dollars, one way. My last trip was three hundred fifty dollars, one way. Most of my life I have had my own company, different professions, but mostly mine. When I have to check a box on a form, I check "retired," but I still go up and see clients I have worked with before and work with a friend who is in real-estate investment in the Bay Area. But down here, I would say I am ninety percent retired. Most of the people I worked with became friends, so I go to visit family and friends there. I have three sons, the second birth being identical twins.

MS. I can hardly imagine you carrying twins!

I found this truly astounding because Zandra was thin and slight. Her tiny face had blue eyes accented by dark makeup. She was always dressed immaculately, like she was on her way to the city to discuss creative solutions concerning beauty and function. People carry their histories with them in the way they dress and in other habits of a lifetime. Until writing these interviews, I never asked people why they lived here for fear of answers like the Witness Protection Program or a fugitive status. "That's why God made Mexico" as the song goes.

Zandra smiled and added, "I was like a small elephant. They each weighed seven point two pounds. It was a natural birth."

MS. What were you eating while they were in utero? Lots of minerals to build bones?

ZF. Anything I wanted. Sort of like the pickles and peanut-butter diet but with Mexican and Chinese food. I ate what I craved.

MS. So if you are not working here, what do you do with your time?

ZF. I try to read as much as I can. I watch movies on the computer. I don't have a TV; I'm a movie freak. I give back to the community by doing volunteer work. I also spend time keeping in touch with friends all over the world. Up north, I volunteered every Friday at the Marine Mammal Center. Since the sea mammals are healthy down here, I transferred my care for animals to the turtle-nesting projects and the spay and neuter clinics.

After Hurricane Odile, I began working more for organizations involved in the children of Todos Santos. I've been helping out with the Internado and the CAM school right next door, which serves people with special needs. They help people between the ages of six months and sixty years of age. Everyone seems to want to help, although we don't raise huge amounts like other fundraising endeavors. I've volunteered at the Historic House Tour and the music festival, which are both sponsored by the Palapa Society to help the children of the town through school scholarships and medical funding. I have a new project about art for the town children, not just the Palapa children, but I can't talk about it yet.

MS. It seems like you facilitate a lot of fun things, like restaurant openings. Do you just walk in the door and say, "This looks like fun; need some help putting on an event?"

Zandra laughed at that image of herself and said, "Remember the nice Mother's Day event at the Uruapan Restaurant where we each had to wear something from Nancy's *segunda?*"

"*Segunda*" means second, so Nancy's is a secondhand store called *Tesoro Escondido* [Hidden Treasure], which has stylish, consignment, gringa clothes and lots more.

Zandra continued, "Thirty-five people came, even a few guys. There were door prices for wearing more than one item from Nancy's. Believe it or not, two women got into a high school cat fight because they thought they each should have won. I wanted to do something fun for Nancy, a generous, kind, loving human being whose *segunda* had once been housed in the restaurant space where we had the event. I had met the younger chef and his family and wanted to help them get some ideas for attracting more business. We are friends and share time together."

MS. So you just keep your eyes and ears open for ways you can help bring the community together?

ZF. Well, sometimes you have these feelings you have known people before. I had that feeling about you when I first met you.

We were going to go to Buena Fortuna in La Ribera on the east side of the peninsula.

I had been to Buena Fortuna 3 times to meet and mine the encyclopedic mind of Gabriel Howearth, a seed collector, who has brought many species from around the world to his land in Baja. He was the originator of Seeds of Change, an early company specializing in true seeds, no hybrids. He is an incredible resource. He and his partner in the project, Kitzia Kokopehmana, conduct tours in the winter season which include a delicious meal from their garden. I am always encouraging others to visit this botanical garden in our area. There are many mature trees of the tropic zone you may never see unless you travel the tropics world wide including the south pacific islands. He also has an aloe vera garden with thirty-plus varieties, all from Africa. Zandra and I have talked of going together every winter, but so far haven't gone.

MS. It's not over yet. Maybe we'll get there this winter. Have you ever been to the cactus sanctuary near El Triunfo?

ZF. Oh, yes! I always take my guests there.

My admiration for Zandra—this modern, black and white, crispy-clean lady—was growing, because the sanctuary is not a Disney production with asphalt walking paths. It is more like an old-growth desert forest, dense and overgrown, just like nature does it in the Baja. Cactus and trees hug each other, because one is fixing nitrogen in the soil and the other is providing shade, and they are both holding water in the soil with their roots. One can see some very old specimens of endemic plants.

MS. Tell us a little about buying your lot and building on it.

ZF. I wasn't going to buy raw land. This was raw land. I was working twenty-four-seven up north; I wasn't thinking of building. The last place we went to that day of looking was this land. We walked on the dunes, down to the beach. My friend said, "Buy this land!" I said, "No. There's nothing on it!"

Back in northern California, I met the people who owned it, and they made an offer I couldn't refuse. This is the lifestyle I want to live. One of my favorite places I'd lived in my past was a houseboat in Sausalito. I lived in Sausalito for twenty-five years, including ten years in a little town called Bolinas, where I raised my kids. So I bought the property. [*She had a hardy laugh at the memory.*]

It started out that I would live downstairs and have a roof deck, but there was no view of the ocean from below. I told the contractor, "We're going to go up." I knew I would never live downstairs. I met with the engineer and created this small apartment up here with the big deck so it would feel like a houseboat. The top floor was finished first, and the bottom just completed four and a half years ago. It is about one thousand one hundred square feet. And this top half is about five hundred square feet. I like living in a small space. It's like a combination loft and houseboat.

MS. How long has the first floor been a rental? And how is it working out?

ZF. I now rent short term—one, two, or three weeks only. Last season I had a year-long renter, and I wasn't comfortable being a caretaker. As a guest or a visitor, you are in awe, but long term becomes a little more demanding.

MS. Do you see yourself living in the north again?

ZF. Never. I could never live that lifestyle again. Financially is a big reason. I wake up every morning and can't believe I live here. I love the weather. I love it.

MS. What are your challenges down here?

ZF. I miss my family and friends north. I'm very close to my friends, and they do come down to visit. I'm not on Facebook, because I'm a compulsive worker and don't want to spend much time on the computer. As it is, I average one and a half hours a day, not counting movie time.

MS. Is Spanish a challenge?

ZF. Yes. Every year I say I am going to take another Spanish class, and I don't. But I will. My comprehension is pretty good. But I don't get the words out in the right order often enough, and I live in the present tense. I have no other tenses. I get around, and I completed the work on the house with the workers in Spanish.

MS. Other challenges?

ZF. My health is better down here. I don't work hard, so there is less stress. What is stressful is living with insects. I hate cockroaches! I've never had to deal with them before. I attack the cockroaches with a broom, so we are far from each other. Once while I was staying in town, there was a mother scorpion and her babies in my suitcase. I had to get someone to help me. I would never before put DEET on my skin. Now I'm older, and I do. Don't like spiders, either. But I look at it now as a strength I have acquired. I also need a do-it guy. I can't live without one. After all my experience with builders in the Bay Area, where everything must be perfectly square, the work ethic here was an adjustment. Here when it is finished, when you plug in a light and it turns on, you celebrate. I will admit I had four meltdowns with the workers. But I'd say today that is ninety-five percent gone from my personality.

MS. Do you feel like you have integrated at all into the Mexican culture?

ZF. Somewhat. We are all guests and visitors here. We always will be. We should just respect everyone. In the first Palapa Society walk-run fund raiser, I walked through the barrios on the route and was astounded how many people knew me and called out my name. After Odile, one of the original workers on the house walked all the way out from town to check on me. That's the kind of community we live in. I didn't pick Todos Santos; Todos Santos picked me. In 1990, my friends and I walked into the old theater on the plaza, and they said, "You are going to do festivals here, and you are going to live here forever." There was something here that had a magnet attached to me, though I didn't return for twelve years.

MS. How did Hurricane Odile affect you?

ZF. It definitely made me closer to my community. I want to help the kids. I was here for the event...downstairs with my cats. I was scared for my life. The glass doors up here got hit by debris and looked like they had been sliced with a knife. There was a lot of water and cleanup, but nothing compared to what happened to others. I want to be down here for the hurricane season, though I hope we don't have another category 3-4 storm. I appreciate the strength of cement and rebar after seeing all the damage Odile brought us.

MS. I notice a lot of books stacked by the bed. What do you like to read?

ZF. They are there because someone is modifying the bookcase by the door. I had never read a detective novel in my life before moving here. Now I love them. As much as I like technology, I don't have a Kindle. I like to have the book in my hand. I love and adore books. I rely on the Palapa library, and I have a friend who has a great library and is always supplying me with books. Also when people leave, they pass along books. That's one of the joys of being retired. Oh, and there's a mah-jongg group, which meets every Monday at a restaurant. It's fun and tactile and a little thought to it.

I have always been a people person. I was an only child, so I grew up around adults in very social communities. My parents always had dinner parties. From an early age, I had a social life. I've always seen what I do as involving other people in a project, whatever it is. Delegate work to competent or incompetent people. It's like a party. Life is like a big party!

I have such good friends here. Someone will come and help if I need it. We all live relatively close together, and that alone creates community. I used to have a much different vision of myself, because up there, I had a life and a style. I was coming down three or four times a year, and I realized you just don't bring a California lifestyle with you and plop it down in Baja. The house I planned to build here, designed up there, was way too big. I'm so glad I didn't build it.

The decision to live full-time here was sort of made for me by the crash in real estate. Everything was going flat. I got out just in time. Todos Santos is one of the best places for a mature woman to live—psychically, physically, mentally, spiritually. All of it. Because whatever you want in your life, you can find here. Eating out, book clubs, fabulous library, blockbuster films in La Paz for four dollars instead of twenty dollars up north. I do think of traveling again to Asia, Cambodia, Thailand, and Vietnam.

Zandra and I then spent some time reminiscing about the time she helped me organize a Valentine's Day party at my casa. I hired four serenade singers with their acoustic instruments, and they entertained some seventy people for hours on a Valentine's night with a perfect temperature. There were food and drink, tables and benches, and my store, the Tiny Tienda, was the hub of the action.

Valma and Nancy brought red, pink, and white clothes to sell. Anita brought her jewelry. Laurie had hung her marvelous photographs, and Carol displayed her art cards. We all made sales, and people drifted in and out with the music. The top deck was full of lounge chairs, where people told me later they reclined and soaked up the love songs.

Zandra was a big help to me in her suggestions and encouragement. She showed up for a few hours of set up even though she had to drive to San Jose to pick up her guests. She told me later that people still talked about that party: "It was the best one of the year!"

Thank you, Zandra, for being who you are!

CHAPTER 13

PICKLE DAY

Pickle Day lived a short walk over the dunes to a favorite surf break of the Southern Baja surfers called La Pastora. She started surfing at age twenty-six in San Diego, California, and now at fifty-four, she was taking a break after back surgery on a herniated disc six weeks prior. I had to ask her how she came by the name Pickle.

She said, "I was waitressing and learning to surf from the busboys. I would hardly ever be out of the water, and my skin was always wrinkled. So the busboys at the Spaghetti Factory started calling me Pickle. And it has stuck."

Pickle lived in a classic Airstream trailer (twenty-nine feet by eight feet) called a Land Yacht, so said a steel plate attached by the door. It was situated under a big *palapa*, newly built after Hurricane Odile crashed her older, smaller one down on the Airstream with just cosmetic damage. She thought that the old *palapa* roof lying on the trailer during the storm actually saved the trailer from more damage and saved the solar-powered refrigerator and freezer she had out back of it. The high winds moved the Airstream off its jacks and set it down two feet off the cement pads while she spent the storm snug in her neighbor's adobe house.

The new *palapa* was eight meters by ten meters (that is twenty-six feet by thirty-two and one-half feet). Bigger and stronger than the first *palapa*, the rebuilt offered plenty of shaded and protected space for life outside the trailer. It cost her $10,000 to have it built after Odile, including new posts set in cement. The builder gave her that bid before all material prices went up, so she was not sure if the worker made a reasonable profit for his labor. Along with the *palapa*, she built an outbuilding that housed the bathroom, shower, surfboards, and storage, for when she wants to save things under a roof during a hurricane or tropical storm. Built into the outside wall were a sink and a *lavatorio* [a cement sink and side-board for doing laundry].

We were sitting under the tightly woven palapa, admiring it and the classic lines of the Airstream, when Pickle said, "I'm pretty set and comfortable."

MS. How did you come by the trailer?

Pickles Day (PD). It belonged to a brother of a friend who drove it down and parked it on an empty lot in the desert seven miles from Todos Santos. When I bought it, it had been broken into many times, and a lot of the inside was gone. Plus there was black mold on the walls and everywhere else. I paid one thousand dollars and then did a work trade for another one thousand dollars. I gutted it the rest of the way and redesigned the inside to suit my needs. I love it. [*It is indeed roomy and functional.*]

I don't spend a lot of daylight hours in it, but I do sleep in it now. I used to sleep outside on a cot. But every summer a rattle-snake comes and lives under the fridge or the trailer, and I didn't want to step on it during the night. One of my dogs [*out of three*] sleeps on the cot now, and I am glad he is off the ground, out of harm's way.

MS. How did you get to Mexico?

PD. While living in San Diego, I crossed the border often to surf at k-thirty-eight [*That's kilometer thirty-eight*] Baja Highway One.

On weekdays, there was no one surfing, and I didn't have to be at work until four thirty. So I went every day. In fact I crossed the border so often that they eventually searched my car and me for guns and drugs. Nada. Do I look like a gunrunner?

Pickle was five-foot one inch tall with midback-long hair in five shades of blond, bronze, and brown. There was a cackle in her laugh, and her speaking voice was sometimes too loud for the distance between us. Maybe it was a habit from talking over crashing waves.

MS. Did you just fall in love with surfing and become addicted?

PD. Yeah, I've never been a beach bunny, someone who just sits on the beach. I have always been active—dancing, gymnastics, exercise. So surfing was a natural thing for me to fall into.

MS. How did you get to Baja Sur?

PD. I wanted to leave California because I was partying too much. I got into drugs, and I wanted out. I got a van, camping gear, and a dog and drove down to Scorpion Bay and heard about the great surf break at Todos Santos. So I drove down in 1993. I just surfed that winter, because the plan was to go down the coast of Mexico surfing. I went all the way down to Oaxaca, surfing the whole way. I stayed in Mexico for a year. Then I went back to the United States, and in a short time, I was back in Chiapas teaching English at a private English-language school, Harmon Hall. The fourteen-hour days were tough, and I lasted four months. It was a six-hour drive to a point-break surf area, but there was lots of wind. So it wasn't the best bet to find a good day to drive all that way.

MS. Did you have a degree in English as a second language?

PD. No. I had a BA in communications from the University of Iowa. That's all you needed to teach English. They put me through a training course, which was two weeks long, not much. The whole thing was stressful. The classes were two hours long, and then a break to plan the next class. I met an American surfer who was going to Costa Rica to surf, so we made a plan to go at Christmas break. But the school said no break! No substitute teacher. I had to go. So I quit. It was my one chance to surf through Central America. And we did, all the way to Costa Rica.

MS. I guess you knew your priorities. What happened after Costa Rica?

PD. I had been living in Mexico, so all my money was in pesos. I was in El Salvador at the time that the peso was devalued by one-half. That wiped out my savings. I had to get back to the United States and make money. I ran out of money in Todos Santos. While I was camping out by La Pastora, there was a construction site in progress, and I got a job caretaking the site while the builders were gone. It was 1994. I watered and weeded and did site maintenance. There was nothing out here then, and it turned into five years of camping and surfing. It was a lucky break to even find a job in surfer's paradise. I was probably thirty-five at the time.

MS. Did you go back to the States?

PD. I did. I went to the Ventura-Oxnard area and worked in restaurants and saved money to come back. You can make good money in the right restaurant if you are frugal and a good saver, a good budgeter, which I am. I don't eat much, and I'm always at the beach, which doesn't cost anything. It was tough readjusting to life in California after so many years in Mexico. Truth be told, it was horrible.

I came down to Todos in the winters of 2002 and 2003, and then in 2004, I was here to stay. I always came back to this neighborhood. This is where I have always lived in Todos. In February 2005, I started caretaking five acres north of here. In the spring and summers, I would go to the east-cape region to surf when a swell came up. Places like Shipwreck. But I can't tell you the names of other places because surfers would kill me. They don't like crowded waves. They keep their favorite breaks a secret.

MS. How long have you been in this spot?

PD. The five acres where I lived and caretook had five owners, and one year they all came down at different times. I had enjoyed being there solo and thought I should leave the property when any of the owners showed up. I was always moving off and then back on. That proved to me that I wanted a more permanent living arrangement. In 2007 or 2008, the owner of the Airstream and the owner of the land got together and agreed that I could park the trailer here and live in exchange for property maintenance, weeding, watering, checking up on things, because the owners are only here three to four months a year. So I pay no rent, but that could change when they come down to live full-time. The surfing community is a good one: people helping and looking out for each other.

Nothing ever stays the same, though. Life is always in flux, and things change so fast sometimes. I cannot and don't want to do the landscape maintenance I have done as work exchange and money for the past ten years. Five years ago, I was sore all the time from weeding, which can be overwhelming after a rainy fall. Bent-back labor is too much for me at fifty-four.

I may pay rent someday. Right now I am selling organic produce at a good location in Todos Santos. My hours just got cut way back from five to two days a week, because the winter people have left and sales are down. I worked for Ross, my neighbor, for three years selling his organic produce at my own stand at the end of your street!

That was how I first met Pickle, because I am no surfer! Ross had been growing organic vegetables and herbs for export to the United States for thirty-some years.

MS. How much would you say you live on a month?

PD. I just figured that out because I had to. Twelve thousand pesos a month. At today's rate of exchange, that is about seven hundred dollars a month, but it fluctuates all the time.

MS. What are you going to replace land maintenance with for an income?

PD. I have started a pet-care service: walking dogs, feeding pets, and so on. I have people asking me if I can spend the night while they stay in Cabo. I have to figure out the value of this. And I'm going to charge in US dollars, because the peso goes up and down constantly. Maybe fifteen dollars an hour for dog walking, fifty dollars for overnights. I mean, I'm leaving my house and my animals alone for the night.

[*A year after the interview I talked to Pickle, who said that she had stayed nights one week at a pet-care assignment and when she returned home, a rat had moved into her trailer. It took her many attempts in a week's time to get the rat out—finally in a gopher trap.*]

MS. What are some of the things you have learned here, and how have you grown from the experience?

PD. You have to learn how to live here. There are such extremes: the heat in summer, the cold wind in the winter, the insects and snakes, the hurricanes and other wind events. You have to be able to move around your structure: be on the south side in the winter when it's cold and the north side in the summer when it's hot.

If you are off the grid, you have to figure out the solar thing. Now I have four panels. The refrigerator and freezer each have their own panel and battery, and I have two for the trailer so I can run fans in the summer. They are mounted in the air on tilting frames for the angle of the sun, but I have to take them down when a hurricane comes. I can't do it myself, so I have to hire someone to help me. One way I've grown here is acquiring patience. Here it is two steps forward, one step back. It's always a series of trade-offs. I've learned it's best not to get angry.

MS. Do you speak Spanish?

PD. Yes. I have taken Spanish in school since I was in grammar school, all through high school and college. I do fine and can carry on a conversation.

MS. Have you integrated into the Mexican community?

PD. I haven't integrated into any culture. I'm really a loner. I don't like large groups and prefer one-on-one situations. No parties. I like dogs best. I find male relationships complicated and don't desire one. I socialize while I'm selling produce, but those are short encounters.

MS. You have a great laugh, so I'm glad you share your spark with others over the spinach and papayas. Does your family ever come down?

PD. I've met my younger brother once in Puerto Vallarta and twice in Cabo San Lucas. And his two daughters, who are now in their twenties, came with him. It was fun.

MS. Do you have plans for the future?

PD. I'm a little bored here right now. I think I miss the freedom of moving around now that I have day jobs. My days had always been free, time-wise. Also I'm bored because of too much domestication, being settled in with a trailer and this expensive roof. I'm a little bored with Pastora surf break after all these years. And I'm always worried about money. It is so hard to make money down here. I've had the rug pulled out from underneath me five times.

I would like to live here maybe five more years and then see what and where I want to go. Mainland Mexico seems risky to me now, even traveling there. In some towns, the narcos come in, and the town shuts down and caters to them. Plus, it is getting really crowded on the mainland. I would have to pick my time of year to travel. My family still owns seventeen acres in Iowa that I could live on…in the middle of a cornfield. *Depserata* script, that one, but you never know the future. I know I will probably always have to work.

MS. Are there challenges for you living here?

PD. Right now recovering from the disc operation, I am challenged by my camping lifestyle—moving the heavy water containers and the big propane tanks. I have lived a glorified camping life for years, and it might have to phase out as I get older. It's becoming physically challenging. It's so physical down here. Never expected that consequence of getting older.

I have to share the sign by Pickle's door to the Land Yacht: "Beware of attack gecko." She pointed out the handicraft tin gecko in bright colors just inside the door and flashed me a big grin.

Good luck, my friend with all your decisions and happy healing!

CHAPTER 14

ANITA TRAMMELL

Anita lived in Colonia Las Brisas. Her gate was big, metal, and painted stark white, with a gigantic red hibiscus flower covering almost the entire surface. I was greeted by a friendly, furry, short dog, Viva, and a bigger, black dog named Sugar. Anita was soon to follow; she was wearing a loose, flowing dress of many colors, with the hem short enough for me to glimpse her shapely legs. I had noticed them before because they were a true asset. They sort of balanced out the immense energy coming from her engaged face. Short, brown hair crowned her head, and a white, toothy smile welcomed me to the land and house that she was leasing to buy.

We walked around her land, maybe a half acre, talking plants and seeing the different areas that had already been there and the ones she had added. Being a permaculturist myself, I love plants and people who love plants. On our walk, I noticed a large tray of quartz crystals and then another one, equally as large, at another corner of the house.

Anita said, "I have spent years digging crystals from an open-pit crystal mine in Hot Springs, Arkansas."

In the house were bowls of crystals and a bookcase filled with treasures from the earth: a prehistoric rock tool and a rock with a drilled hole probably used for starting fire, plus unusual rocks that make you want to touch them and wonder about their origins.

"I'm a regular rock hound. I see beauty in all God's creations," she said as she cradled a rock in her hands.

The house she nows calls home was small with spacious kitchen, living room with table, and a separate building for the bedroom and bathroom. It looks like the people who built it hadn't taken it to refinement level, so Anita made some wonderful additions to the kitchen's efficiency. The lot had a free flow view to the ocean with lots of green growing things waving back at you and very few houses.

Anita came to Todos Santos two years ago from Texas. She was now fifty-five years young and had a beautiful complexion. She had lived all over Texas and graduated from the University of Texas at Austin with a degree in art, after starting out in math. While in school, she did studio painting, watercolor, and all the other mediums for painting, plus silk screening and silver jewelry. At the moment, the tools of her creative talents were scattered on the top of her only table and she swept them away so we could enjoy a cup of tea as we talked about her life as it was before she came to the Baja.

MS. Tell me how you decided to come to Mexico and start a new life.

Anita Trammell (AT). After graduating from college, I entered the job market and pretty much dropped the art. I worked in the office of Southwest Airlines for twenty-one and a half years, sixteen of that working on computers, scheduling pilots for training programs. The last ten years, I worked for a woman much like myself, only too stubborn to let me carry the new programs on the computer to new heights of flexibility so more programs could be added later. We fought all the time. And my big mouth got me in all kinds of trouble.

I have been an alcoholic most of my life, as other members of my family have been before me. Also I was diagnosed with bipolar disorder at forty-eight. My doctor and I tried every combination of medication to stabilize my mood swings. The next step would have been shock treatments. No! [*Her eyes were big, and her mouth was in a perfect oval.*] I'm considered a functioning bipolar personality. I can lash out with a fierce temper sometimes. I started learning how to not take things so personally. I learned a lot from AA, which I attended for years.

At one point I drank a case of beer and smoked a joint on the fourteen-mile drive home and rolled the car end over end and suffered a head injury, no doubt contributing to the bipolar imbalance of the brain. At work I made so many mistakes because I would work for eight hours, then stay up until midnight doing art, sleep four hours, and then go to work. Once I was receiving a training, and I fell asleep as the woman was talking. Bipolar people need sleep.

The stress on the job was so high that they were about to fire me, so I took a family medical leave and went into rehab. If I hadn't gone into rehab, they would have fired me, and I would have lost my lifetime flight benefits, which I had worked really hard for. After three months, I went back to work but continued to make too many mistakes. I started looking around for a place to go, to change my life. The job was killing, shingles, bleeding ulcers, and an anxiety attack at work. I was looking on the East Coast, the Caribbean area, when a friend told me about Todos Santos, a little art colony in southern Baja where I could get back to my art.

I went home, looked on Craigslist, and found a house to rent in Las Tunas. Upon calling the owner, I was told that I was twelfth on the list. I asked, "What would get me to the top of the list?" She said, "Send the money," which I did immediately. I was on my way to Mexico six weeks later. I had an estate sale and bought a six-by-ten trailer. A friend, Becky, drove down with me. She was fluent in Spanish, so that was a relief to my family. I didn't speak any Spanish.

MS. Did you have doubts? Has spontaneity always been a part of your personality?

AT. Oh, yes! And never a doubt…this is what I need to do.

MS. How did your family and friends react?

AT. I was either crazy, or they were really envious. My father was angry, and my mother went around crying because I was going to get my head chopped off. I said to her, "No, Mom. This isn't a border town." My dad would write scathing e-mails to me. They almost got a divorce over it. Dad started carrying a gun around in his pocket. And I'm saying, "You always wanted me to grow up, so now I am growing up!" My mother has come down twice and seen how beautiful it is; hopefully my dad will come one day.

MS. How was the transition? Were there adventures?

AT. Every day is an adventure, but no big ones on the way. It was June, and there were flowers everywhere, a different color on the other side of every hill. We had fun. I drove in to Todos Santos sight unseen and loved it. Three weeks after arriving, the transmission went out on my car. That was my first bad mechanic experience, taking advantage of a gringa. But all of us emigrants crawl through that con game at least once.

MS. I like to think that in Mexico there are three prices: one for the Mexicans, one for the gringo, and another for the gringa. Were you discouraged by that?

AT. No. The one time I got discouraged was when my purse got stolen right out of this house with all my ID, credit cards, cash, passport, phone, camera, and car keys. It happened the day I came to put a deposit on it. We were in the back of the lot when someone entered the front and stole it. I am now in the process of buying the land and house, and it should be paid off in five years. The house definitely has potential. There are two outdoor terraces which could be the start of a guest room and a bedroom, and turn the present, stand-alone bedroom into a workshop. I could use one, don't ya think? (We grinned as we looked around the living room cluttered with canvases here and there, piles of fabric draped over wire lampshades, little side tables and trays waiting to be painted in nature motifs, and the TV silently dramatizing life in another era.)

MS. You always have ideas and plans it seems, and that, like me, you collect raw materials with which to create.

AT. I guess you could say I'm a type-A personality. All my friends are, too.

It was a big self-esteem builder to come here and be successful with my art. I never considered myself an artist or a very good one. But now I have stepped forward and can say, "I am an artist." And I'm doing OK.

MS. Was opening a shop in town a snap decision?

AT. More like a spree. There was an empty room behind the bookstore that was available for rent. I took it. For my first year here, I went to markets in Cabo San Lucas, Todos Santos, Los Barillas, La Paz, and Baja Beans, in Pescadero, trying to find a venue for my jewelry and art.

I first met Anita at Baja Beans' Sunday market, where I was selling also. She was immediately friendly and warm, like we'd been friends before. I thought she had been in the area for a while, but, no, she was new. She just had a gregarious personality and a gift of gab, and she seemed to trust people immediately.

AT. Doing the markets in Cabo San Lucas three days a week was hard because I had to leave at five in the morning and drive long distances. The cost of gas was a consideration. I called my accountant to figure if I could afford the rent for the shop. He said. "Go for it!" Now I get to do what I love all day. I call the shop Casita Anita.

MS. What do you sell in the shop?

AT. My paintings and lots of beaded jewelry, which I love to create. I have thousands of beads. Part of my manic is love of shopping. I make mobiles out of sea glass, cactus pincushions, and crocheted pitcher covers. I buy furniture from the *segundas*, which I paint in all kinds of creative motifs. Here is one I am going to paint a scrabble board on. Also I do consignment for other crafters and a dress designer, Pepita, from Cabo.

MS. She's the partner in the fashion show you did last winter.

AT. Yes. She's had a dress shop in Cabo San Lucas for twenty-seven years called Magic of the Moon. Great styles! We went in together on the fashion show—her clothes, my jewelry. It was her idea to have regular people be the models—short, round, tall, skinny. The idea being, "You, too, would look beautiful in these clothes just like these (extra)ordinary women."

MS. Was it successful?

AT. We set up in a lovely outdoor terraced restaurant, and the models went to each table, instead of having a runway. The audience loved seeing their friends modeling the fantastic clothes. It was a huge networking event for me. So many people discovered my store from that event.

MS. You have such panache! I love walking into your shop. There is so much to see, textures to delight in. I love how you get an idea, and bingo, it's a ball rolling toward a goal.

AT. I love stepping out and doing different things. I guess I'm a natural risk taker.

MS. You help people put together necklaces and earrings, don't you?

AT. Yes, and change out clasps and refurbish old jewelry, as well as sell jewelry supplies and my amazing bead collection.

MS. What's it like having a shop almost on Main Street?

AT. Actually I am moving to Main Street next month. Look for the turquoise building "Casita Anita" on Calle H. Colegio Militar. I love working in the store because I meet so many people. I have never been a stranger, always a people person.

MS. What are your observations of the Mexicans and their culture?

AT. They have their priorities straight; family is first. And they are self-sufficient. For years, this town was isolated, and people did for themselves and helped each other out. I like that it is a close-knit community. Mexicans are ingenious inventors. They can find a solution or make a tool from what is lying around. I wish the Mexicans would participate more in the recycling and other gringo-inspired events, but that's OK.

MS. Do you feel like you have integrated much into the Mexican community?

AT. Not really. I need to know the language. I took one class for a month, three times a week. Now it is suspended because people have left.

At this point Anita and I wailed on about our Spanish-learning experiences: too much useless vocabulary like "socks," too many verbs every day to overload the brain, needing reviews instead of more words. Better to have a class where you can ask for a Spanish word you're going to need tomorrow when you go to the whatever office or a phrase you could have used yesterday.

MS. Do you take an interpreter with you sometimes?

AT. Yes, but sometimes friends don't want to come because they want me to learn it! I've been lucky to find doctors who speak English because they studied in the States. I'm getting together with a friend once a week to review so we don't lose what we have, and we'll be ready to go again when the high season brings in the money to pay for a class.

MS. How much money do you spend a month?

AT. About two thousand dollars, because I have the two rents and then what everyone else pays for—propane, Wi-Fi, electric, water. I like to eat out but can't do it too often. There are lots of fun things to do that don't take money, like playing scrabble and having friends over to watch a movie.

MS. So you like it so much you are buying this house.

AT. Yes. It is what I was looking for. The mountains and the ocean, it's my idea of paradise. But I feel the risk of living here with the hurricane inevitability, the threat of the gold mine in the sierras threatening the water source, the cartel violence that shook the town last fall. But I love it here. It's like living in the fifties when you see someone ride a horse into town. You have to be a bubble off to live here. It isn't for everybody.

MS. Are there challenges here for you?

AT. The same as in the United States: buying beyond my means. I get depressed and want to buy something.

MS. What do you buy here?

AT. Pottery, fabric, everything! And of course, it is challenging to figure out the way the Mexican mind works, like the roadwork that has torn up the town and left the main street looking like a dusty frontier town. No signage to tell you not to go down this street, and then no exit at the end of the street—just a huge hole or a mountain of dirt, causing you and others to have to back up all the way to where you entered. I'll never figure it out why they don't put up a sign: no exit/*no salida* or no entrance/*no entrada*.

MS. What about your love life? Any?

AT. None, but that's all right with me. My picker is broken; I make terrible choices for partners. I never wanted to have kids because of my family history of alcoholism. I've been alone for twenty years, and I'm in the rut of doing what I want to do when I want to do it. I don't know if I could incorporate another person in my life.

After the interview and the recorder was turned off, Anita told me an amazing story from her life. When she was twelve, her family moved to England because of her father's work. From the sixth through the ninth grades, she attended a school where one weekend every month was a three-day weekend and a group of students would venture out into the world with a professor of some expertise. They went throughout Europe to Austria, Germany, northern Italy, England, and Eastern Europe. She saw the world with good guidance from someone who knew what the group had come to see and what they all were looking at.

When she spoke of the time, her tone was reverent and calm and respectful of the beautiful memories. It was an incredible learning experience for her, instilling a love of travel and history, which has made her inquisitive and brave, unafraid to experience new things.

Anita said, "Some of my first jobs were as a travel agent and working for National Car Rental at an airport. I just wanted to be around that traveling energy."

During our interview, Anita would wander down what she called "rabbit trails." All of these stories had details galore that flipped back and forth through time. Then she would stop herself and say, "Well, that's another rabbit trail," as if knowing that she was way off course. She must have said it four times. We would still be talking if I hadn't pulled us back to the topic at hand. Her mind might never stop.

A little while ago, I hired Anita to show me some methods and tricks on my computer. I was struck by the immense mental energy coming from her brain. Synapses firing, patterns running, possibilities coming into focus. It seemed like her whole creative life was like that. A million ideas and a powerful force to manifest them. She might be manic, but it is a wave to ride on when she inspired me and others to create our dreams. We are lucky to have her as a resident and contributor to our community.

CHAPTER 15

ANITA HARRIS

Anita lived a five-minute walk over a sand dune to the beach. She lived with a horse, four dogs, and a cat. The first greeter was Hombre, the horse. He came to his corral fence to welcome me and check me out. I knew he would be here, because Anita had shared the news of deciding to keep him at home instead of at a corral a drive away. The next greeters were two big dogs and then one little dog and then Anita herself, in a black-velvet tank top and printed tights showing off her slim legs and body. I wasn't jealous, just envious. I saw that the pink bangs on the spiky hairdo had faded a little since the last time I saw her, but her new tattoo had not faded in the least.

Anita's house was a spacious one bedroom filled with furniture for herself and the dogs and art canvases she had painted. We immediately moved to the balcony off the dining room to see Hombre's new shade structure, necessary for the hot months ahead. It was obvious that he had ample space and a huge place in Anita's heart. When I put my hand down to pet him, he curled back his great horse lips, revealing green-yellow teeth. A smile? I quickly withdrew my hand, but Anita was right there offering what he expected. A biscuit treat. Now we were all happy.

We sat at a round table filled with a life well lived and got down to the story of her arrival in Baja from England. Her boss at an import-export company in England where she had worked for many years had a son who moved to La Paz, the capital of Baja California Sur, some forty miles from Todos Santos, on the Sea of Cortez side of the peninsula. There he started the Cortez Club, which offered adventures in the La Paz Bay—things like scuba diving, swimming with whale sharks, sea lions, and more. She and her boss, the father, came to La Paz to check it out and completely fell in love with La Paz.

Anita said, "I returned several times on vacation and stayed in the house with the employees of the club. I met more people who asked me, 'Why don't you come live here?' I said, 'Oh, I couldn't! I couldn't!'"

But back in England she talked about it so much that her co-workers named it for her: "my dream." In January 2000, she said, "It was raining. I was huddled around a fire all bundled up in sweaters and realized that I didn't want to be doing this in five years' time. 'What am I going to do?' I asked myself. The next day at the office a friend asked, 'What are you doing about your dream?' Well, nothing. He then asked if I had put my house on the market. Well, not yet. He said, 'Nothing is going to happen until you do that. Let's go ring the agent.' This was in February. By September, I was in La Paz with a suitcase and a duffel. The house sold right away. I sold all the furniture."

MS. That seemed to be an affirmation from the universe that it was the right decision. Did you have any doubts?

Anita Harris (AH). Not then, because there was so much to do and all the excitement of having a new life. But my friends were full of doubts. I knew I could come back if it was a mistake. They're not going to shut the gate to England and say I can't come back. The doubt hit me six months later while walking back from the *malecon*. I asked myself, "What have you done? What have you done? You don't even speak the language." [*The malecon is the wide breakwater-strolling path, which happens to be the longest one in Mexico. Before the technological take-over of everyone's spare time, the* malecon *was the meeting place for friends and relations. This* malecon *has beautiful modern sculptures and a curving motif in the paving bricks encouraging you to stroll on.*]

And then there was Dorian's, a department store, which was so old-fashioned. Living in London, I was in stores like John Lewis, Selfridge's, an occasional trip to Harvey Nichols. I stood in Dorian's and said. "This is it. Back to the fifties. Whatever you've done, Anita, get used to it."

[*Anita had a grand laugh at the memory. She had a ready smile, like one who loved a laugh, be it at herself or someone else.*]

AH. At first I moved back in with the boys from the Cortez Club. But they were young, which was delightful, but they partied a lot and ate the food I'd brought home, like milk for my coffee in the morning. Grr. That lasted only a few weeks, and then I rented a big house. I had a big house in London, so I thought that was what I needed. Not so. Here you don't stay inside all day; you need good outdoor living space.

Of course I was meeting more people by then, gringos and Mexicans. I knew more Spanish, too, and took a two-week course, which was the wrong timing. I'd got in with a crowd who'd go to the tequila bar every night and party. I'd go to class the next morning completely hungover, and I hadn't done the homework. It was a bad start for my Spanish education. I haven't taken classes since. I just talk to people and pick it up.

MS. Wouldn't you need a car living further from downtown?

AH. Yes, I needed a car. I bought a Cherokee Jeep. Someone asked me if I'd bought it to fit in with the Mexicans, so you can see what kind of shape it was in. I had to get a Mexican driver's license to match the plates. A Mexican friend helped me do it. The office is on Calle Colima and is called Transito. So now I had the car parked outside the house, but I was too scared to go anywhere in it because I drove on the other side of the road, on the other side of the car. I thought that was why I bought an old car so that if I bashed it, I wasn't out too much. [*She chuckled at the memory.*]

I always traveled with a map and plotted my course. But I still found myself lost with all the one-way streets, and then I would go back to the *malecon* so I could find my way back. I got to know the town so well that I became a source of information for other people. People love to go to La Paz with me now.

MS. So what was the answer to "Anita, what have you done?"

AH. Well, I guess, you just meet more people, and the new life begins, doing things, going places.

MS. So you didn't come to resume your art or start a new career or some other motivating reason?

AH. No. I came because it seemed like a good idea and I loved the place. I have always loved the sun. This is absolutely ideal for me. I lived in La Paz for six years.

MS. How did you get to Todos Santos?

AH. How I got here is a love story. I was introduced to a horse, and I fell in love with him. We looked into each other's eyes, and I knew I had to buy him.

MS. Had you ever owned a horse?

AH. No.

MS. Had you ever ridden a horse before?

AH. No.

MS. Have you done other things like this in your life? Making snap decisions.

AH. Well, I guess, but they don't seem snap to me. They seem like perfectly logical things to do. It wasn't until later that I realized I had bought a horse. My friends in Todos Santos suggested that I bring the horse here, to their corrals down the street, where they were building a house for themselves. So I came every week-end to ride. This house was for sale, and eventually they bought it, finished it, and lived here while they completed the one on their lot with the corrals. I started looking around for land or a house so I could live close to my beloved Hombre. Meanwhile the friends had finished the house on their land and suggested I buy this one, which was affordable if we did the transaction without a realtor. I've been in this house for eight and a half years. I didn't have to do anything to the house. The guest casita was here also. I love it here.

MS. How do you spend your time?

AH. Every morning at seven, the dogs and I walk to La Pastora, the surf beach two miles from here. [*So the great legs were because she walked four miles on sand every day. I guess I'll just have to be content with the legs I have.*] On Sundays, we're out at six on a horse ride with my friend Penny and her nicely trained horses. There are lovely trails up in the hills from my house. I work two days a week in a shop in town, which sells beautiful, hand-tooled leather purses, glassware, locally made pottery, and art. The owner goes to mainland Mexico and buys once a year. By the way, I'm a citizen of Mexico, so I have the right to work anywhere. That's why I did it. Also I can own my land outright. I have the deed. I didn't need to buy a *fidecomiso* like foreigners have to do. I went to Mexico City twice to get it and worked with a lawyer.

MS. Do you feel like you have integrated well with the Mexican culture?

AH. Todos Santos is a bit different, isn't it? They don't come to the gringo events, but then all the advertising is in English. How would they know? We should go more to their events.

MS. This is my first time living in a different culture, but even the cross-cultural events I have been involved with in the past were difficult. I see that culture is a total thing including everything you think and do and how close you stand and how loud you speak, to whom you speak, what you eat, and when you eat. No way could

I ever be Mexican. At the airport the signs we are to follow say *"extranjeros,"* strangers. We are strange to them, especially to the women, whereas the gardeners and construction workers see, talk, and observe us more than the women do. And we older women living alone with no husband, no children. We are really strange. Though I have been told that you and I are the third migration of single, older women, so they are getting used to the phenomenon.

AH. Yes, that was my experience in La Paz. The Mexicans I rented from constantly asked me where my family was and why didn't I go back and live with the family because that is what they would do. "Why are you here on your own?" What we have to re-member is that Todos Santos is made up of rancheros and fish-ermen. They live on the land, and their parties and dances are there. They don't think to go to the free movies, even if they are Spanish-speaking films made in Mexico. I'm turning into a ranch-era myself! Nothing brings me greater pleasure than to be down there mucking out his corral.

Anita then perked right up and proclaimed that she was an amateur actor and artist. She showed me a painting of a horse on an old blue board, which was what remained of a gate destroyed by the hurricane last fall. On the walls were portraits of all her dogs. She had buried four dogs on her property. Her guard dog, Lobo, had probably deterred thieves; she was the only one on her street who had not been broken into.

Anita chuckled as she said that she had no lessons in art. She said, "Just like horse riding, you buy a horse and get on it." She reminisced that in England she was just an office worker, never stepped out on a limb. "I think I am a whole new person," she said, her eyes wide open.

MS. Tell me about your acting career.

AH. I had never thought of acting. I was a very shy person when I was younger. My parents considered taking me to a speech thera-pist because I never spoke. I remember a first date where I never said a word. When I told my father that I was acting, he simply said, "You?" It has been very challenging, but I wanted to do it. My debut was in a short play, but my glory came as Glinda the Good in a community theater production of the *Wizard of Oz*. I loved Glinda."

Anita and I had some major laughs as we remembered the play. She had improvised a funny scene with Dorothy in the last three performances and was so successful that she was accused of upstaging the principals. Shy no more...more like the imp I was interviewing.

AH. Then I starting working with the local professional actress who had been Dorothy. We did some short plays together in La Paz. If not for her, I probably wouldn't have carried on. We put our heads together, and we did it by ourselves. Last winter we did two short plays to a full house for four nights in Todos Santos. We timed it for the art festival, which happens in February. We are planning a readers' theater for next December. Six actors in all. We have a proper director who is an in-betweeny [*winter person*]. I say gratitudes every day when I look at my life. I feel truly blessed. I could never go back to England.

MS. What about challenges down here?

AH. Every day is a challenge. In England, I never thought where the water came from. How I was using it? Did I have enough? I just turned the tap, and water came out. I had to become aware of my water consumption. Sometimes there is no water to flush the toilet, to wash a plate. I even wrote a letter telling of the trials of it all, had it translated, took it around La Paz, and hand delivered the letters to authorities, even to the mayor. It worked [*meaning they now came more frequently and turned on the valve to her street*]. I go down to the water office now, and they know who I am.

I lived in this house for five years with only solar power. It was challenging just to say to my visitor, "No. You can't use the iron now, only in the daytime when the sun is shining, because you'll draw the battery down and there won't be enough electricity for the evening." And what a giant step into the unknown for me to put oil in the generator [*used for solar backup after several cloudy days or someone plugging in curlers in the evening*]. I've been on the grid for three and a half years now.

Then there is always the language challenge. I guess you get used to the challenges, and you just do them and forget that they are challenges. Hurricanes are always challenging…just living through one, not talking cleanup. I'm just now, nine months later, replacing the roof tiles because the stores were sold out of tiles.

MS. Do you ever get lonely or bored here?

AH. Yes. But it passes. I am by nature not a depressed person.

MS. When you lived in England, did you have tattoos?

AH. One. Now I have six, and I'm about to get another one. Talk about me being spontaneous; when I got my first one, in the office one morning right out of my mouth, I announced I was going to get a tattoo tomorrow. I surprised myself. As I'm driving to the tattoo parlor, my leg started shaking. I talked to myself, "Anita, you don't have to do this. No one is making you do this." The tattoo artist asked me why I had waited so long to get one. I said, "Well, I've always wanted one; how much longer do I have to wait? I'm fifty, and everyone before would say, 'You'll regret it when you're older.' Well, now I'm older, and I still want one. Just get on with it."

MS. How is your love life?

AH. Slim pickings.

MS. What traits of the Mexican people do you admire?

AH. Their friendliness and resilience. No matter what comes at them, they come back on top. They have happy, smiley faces. They don't have much, and they're happy people."

Anita saying this reminded me that I once noticed a happiness survey online including all the nations of the world. Mexico was second for happiness.

AH. There are also traits I dislike. I think it is mostly Todosanteños and not all Mexicans, or else there would be no successful businesses. But they say they are coming and never show, or they come days later and never call to let you know. They are less educated here. Maybe that's why they're happy. The less ya know, ya know? [*She had a big laugh here that I could share in.*] I loved Mexico City. But it is a big city, and people are different there. This is the *campo* [country].

MS. What have you learned about yourself living here?

AH. My own strength surprised me. I did this by myself! I even took scuba-diving lessons. I became a certified diver. It was fabulous, but I am a fair-weather diver. Once, I was down there in murky water, and I became frightened. I saw people come who had a passion for diving, and I told myself I wanted to be passionate about something. Now I have a horse, and he is my passion. That and acting.

I have also turned into a bit of an outdoor freak here. I was never that in England. My morning beach walk is so beautiful. Sometimes I run across a natural turtle hatch, and I help them get to the ocean. And when the whales are cruising by, the walk can take hours. I sometimes ask myself, "What have I done to deserve this? What would I be doing in England if I were there?" None of these things. Probably trying to stay warm.

MS. You have great entertainment value, Anita, something that is nice to have in a friend. Keep up the spontaneity and your love of place, and we'll all smile along with you.

CHAPTER 16

ELIZABETH SUDLOW

E lizabeth Sudlow's house was sheltered behind a solid cement wall, a good dust break on an infamously busy dirt road in the colonia Las Brisas, just a short mile from Todos Santos. The gate is metal and wood with no view to what lies within. Elizabeth opened the gate with a welcoming smile and soft, round, hazel-brown eyes, which I have to say reminded me of a nun's eyes. I don't know why exactly—maybe because they were kind and soft and unadorned.

To the right of the pathway was a construction site, or should I say destruction site: the remaking of a bed frame down to a smaller size. She had made it originally, but she was rethinking her room usage and was using what she had to repurpose the rooms and casitas she already had, plus making a new casita. As I was soon to see on our tour, her future was taking shape as a long-term-rental compound of two studio apartments, an upstairs unit with separate bedroom and eagle-nest terraces, and a two-story, small house at the bottom of her downward-sloping lot.

We entered the house and preceded to the living room, which featured a king-size bed. It was a newcomer to the space, because of all the shuffling of stuff as she created rentals, raised dust, and moved furniture. We sat on the couch and drank some coconut water. She told me that Sudlow was a remake of a Polish name of her emigrant grandfather. Her father was born in the United States, but he was the first to change his name on recommendation of his college professor. She was a second-generation American from Polish descent. The other side of the family arrived much earlier on the *Mayflower.* The United States of America is rich in these stories.

MS. Tell me how you got this far south.

Elizabeth Sudlow (ES). I sailed quite a bit up and down the West Coast on sailboats. I lived in Hawaii for a while and sailed to the South Pacific, and I lived in Australia for six months while I helped a girlfriend build a house. She came here and helped me start this place, but she didn't want to live here. Australia was very expensive. So I would have had to find a job, and that would require me becoming a citizen. It just seemed too far away from family and too expensive to fly back and forth. We broke up, and I stayed on here.

MS. When did you become a boat captain?

ES. In 1986. I was born in Chicago, but my family moved to the West Coast when I was ten. We lived in the little coastal town of Bolinas, California. I graduated early from high school at sixteen and asked my mom if I could leave home. I went to Hawaii with twenty dollars, a backpack, and my surfboard. I had hard times, starving times, and got a job. I was camped on the beach. But there were all these sailboats anchored out, so I would hang out on them and go sailing and discovered that I loved sailing. When I left Hawaii, I decided to build a boat. I went to Port Townsend, Washington, and went to sea school in Seattle. I had logged a lot of hours sailing and working on boats in Hawaii, and I qualified for a one hundred-ton master's license. You have to have a license to get paid to captain a boat, but a master's license is a pretty intense course.

MS. Now to build a boat, was that a big step for you?

ES. Huge! My mother's second husband was a school teacher and carpenter. When we first moved to California we lived on communes in northern California. That's where he developed his carpentry skills, building little, hippie, hobbit houses on the communes. We kids helped him, so I learned some skills. I started building the boat at nineteen. I had met a family on a commune in Hawaii who had built a beautiful boat, a forty-seven-foot ketch. I sailed on it between islands, but they had sailed it to Tahiti. They decided to sail back to the Pacific Northwest, where they had built it, in Port Townsend. So I went with them.

My friend John talked me into building my own boat. My blood father had said that he would fund my college education. But I didn't want to go to college, so I asked him if he would fund the boat project. He had just learned to sail on Lake Michigan and loved the idea. He hired John to help me build the boat. What John and I built was a twenty-seven-foot sloop. We sent away to England for the plans for a famous design called Virtue. Another commune in Port Townsend built the hull, the basic shape of the boat, in a dry-dock situation. We put it upside down and covered it with fiberglass and made it into a plug for a mold.

My boat was the first fiberglass hull made from that mold, and then they made six more after mine. John and I finished it out with wood so it looked like a wooden boat. We glued strips of wood onto the hull and then screwed cedar planks onto that to make it look like a wooden boat from the outside. Then we made a lip of wood on top and screwed on plywood and spruce planks for a deck. The cabin was an African wood called iroko. We made the mast out of spruce, clear-grain, laminated planks, with solid pieces for the bottom and top and crucial junctions for the rigging.

MS. How long did it take you to make it, and how much did it cost?

ES. It took two years, because both John and I had jobs, so we worked off and on. John would set me up with repetitive things to do and taught me like that. It cost thirty-six thousand dollars. Off a showroom floor, that boat would cost over one hundred thousand dollars. Her name was *Bruja*. I sold her eventually. Right now she's up on Ladysmith on Vancouver Island.

I had her down in the marina in La Paz for five years. I lived on her half the year, and the other half, I worked for Outward Bound up in the San Juan Islands, teaching seamanship on twenty-five-foot, dingy-type, wooden oar boats. These were replicas of the long boats used by early seaman because they couldn't bring their big ships into those inland passage ways. They'd safe anchor offshore, and ten men would board these wooden oar boats and be gone for weeks at a time, exploring, mapping, and so on.

MS. How did you get it back to Vancouver? I hear it takes twice as long to go north in the Pacific, and you have to tack west, then east, then west, zigzagging your way north.

ES. I put it on a giant ship that transports boats called *Dockwise*. They sink their boat halfway so that you can drive your boat into a holding tank, which has been measured to your boat's specs, and then underwater welders secure the rack the boat is in to the steel deck below. The water is pumped out, and the boat is secure in a dry dock for the trip. They move many boats on one giant ship and take them all over the world.

I loved that boat, and when I was done with sailing, I never wanted to replace her. She was the one. She only needed one crew member besides me. I could have sailed by myself, but it is safer with two, because you get tired while sailing by yourself. I participated in the Port Townsend Wooden Boat Festival for years. I like the sailing culture, but I got tired of moving around and living on boats. I got tired of being uncomfortable.

MS. Define "uncomfortable."

ES. When you're at sea, one of the biggest accomplishments of the day is *not* falling over. You are always moving, always adjusting. Just putting on your clothes is a challenge, and all pots on the stove have to be clamped in. Constant motion. Not so much when in a marina. Marina life can be described as compressed living. You're surrounded by other people, other boats. Some marinas don't want you to live aboard. Some marinas have a waiting list of three to ten years out to live aboard.

My boat was so small. The cabin floor was maybe twenty-four inches wide by seven feet long and high enough to be able to stand up in. The whole hull was only seven feet wide, so with counters and sink and stove, two people couldn't pass by each other. There was a bucket for a potty. Wash it out really good, and then it was a shower bucket of seawater. In a dock situation, you had to walk whatever distance to the bathroom and shower. If you had a problem, it was a rush!

MS. But you moved other people's boats, too, didn't you?

ES. Yes. The Pacific Northwest is a renowned cruising zone for sailboats because of the beautiful islands and safe anchorage all along. When I was teaching the kids, other sailing folk would see me and ask me if I would sail their boat to Tahiti or somewhere, so I got around for some years. It didn't pay a lot because they were small boats mostly.

MS. Did you have any close calls out on the open ocean?

ES. In the Gulf of Tehuantepec, I was delivering a fifty-seven-foot ketch with a crew of six. Hurricanes are born in that gulf, because it is a junction of the Atlantic and Pacific. High winds can come from the land and blow you out to sea one hundred miles. The recommended way to sail that gulf is to stay one hundred yards from the beach. Even though you may get sandblasted, it is better than being blown out to sea, where the waves build up and can break on top of the boat.

I didn't know that the air intake for the fuel tank was low on one side, and it got underwater and sucked water into the fuel tank and killed the engine. We were about halfway across the gulf when it happened. It was a pretty rough night, but I was able to keep us in the safety zone. We made it across, but we lost the engine. We had a storm jib up and little bit of the mainsail. The wind had dropped, but the swells were big. I tried to fix the engine. It was huge and really hot. The fuel injectors were out, so I couldn't fix it. We were out at sea slopping around like that for five days. I tried flushing the engine out with fuel, but it didn't work. We ended up sailing this wide boat up this tiny, narrow channel in the most southern port in Mexico.

MS. I guess you earned your stripes with that one. Did you have adventures with *Bruja*?

ES. The first trip down the coast in my boat, there were forty-knot winds and twelve- to sixteen-foot waves, and we were literally surfing the waves. The boat would lie over on its side and slide down the face of the wave without tipping over. One person at a time was tied into the life harness on deck, and we would change above and below deck in between wave sets. It took six days from the Puget Sound to San Francisco Bay, which is record time for a boat that size. Normally a boat that size wouldn't surf, but the keel was heavy enough to keep it from going over.

MS. How old were you when you decided to stop living on boats, and why did you decide to disembark here in Todos Santos where there's no marina or calm coastline?

ES. I was forty-six. That's about thirty years of living on boats. I was tired of sailing, and I liked Todos Santos. I liked the feel of the community. Starting in 1989, I would drive down for two or three months in the winter in my VW bus, camping and surfing. I bought this land eleven years ago. I always felt safe and comfortable here. I always felt at home in Todos Santos. The lot is about sixty feet by one hundred twenty feet on a sloping hill, with a wide Pacific view. It had electricity and water to it already and was close to town, and there were mango trees all the way around the periphery.

From the window in the living room, Elizabeth showed me the two-story house at the bottom of her lot. I also saw a big *palapa* that sheltered a Port Townsend city bus Elizabeth had bought and repurposed as an RV. She had driven it down the peninsula to live in on the property while she was building the main house.

A couple of years ago, here at the main house, Elizabeth and a partner would host a home-cooked meal served on the terrace, which was decked out with two long picnic tables. They called it the Yacht Club. Everyone sat together, and there was only one thing on the menu. There was an incredible view of the Pacific, and it was always a sunset event. Many of the same locals came each time, three or four times in a season. It was called a club for tax purposes, and there was a suggested donation. It was a lot of fun. Elizabeth now described it as a social club, because one reason she did it was to meet people. She did it for three years but didn't want to do it anymore.

MS. Any problems with buying the land?

ES. None. The realtor was on the up and up, and there were no problems.

MS. What lessons have you learned while living here?

ES. I've learned to take life more easily and be less critical. The style of craftsmanship here is different from up north. People here have never seen the craftsmanship as they do it up north, so you can't get mad at them for not knowing. Never a problem finding workers. People should know it is going to cost more than they think it will cost. Get used to it; accept it. It's as expensive to build here as in the United States. Now I give bonuses and tips because they are hardly making anything close to what work people make up north. Be generous; don't be an ass.

Life here is less stressful. Families hang together. I don't have close Mexican friends, but I become friends with the people who work for me. I speak Spanish OK. I can understand what is said and have trouble sometimes expressing myself. I never have taken a Spanish class, but I should.

One thing I do like about Mexico, which a lot of people don't like, is the *mordido* system [a bribe] when you get pulled over for a traffic violation. In the States, if you get pulled over, you will get a ticket, and it will be on your record, cost you one to two hundred dollars, and go on your insurance record. Here you can get off the hook for twenty-five dollars, and you'll never see it again. Generally when I've been pulled over here, I was speeding or something. If not, I will argue with them.

MS. What do you do here besides build?

ES. I still surf, and I kite board over in La Ventana in the winter with friends who come down and camp in the camp grounds. It's more like glamping, because they have fancy RVs, but I bring my little tent. We watch movies on a screen strung up on the side of the RV. I like to visit friends here and shop the *segundas* in La Paz. I go back to the States once a year for a month, and I might road trip up every two or three years. I'm a permanent resident now, and I would like to become a citizen. I'm too busy now to study for the test. And I hear they make an allowance in the language part for people over sixty.

MS. How much do you live on a month here?

ES. I can live on five hundred dollars a month. But that doesn't cover repairs and maintenance. One thousand dollars a month is comfortable. Five hundred dollars is doable but barely. All this construction you see—the rental casitas—is to increase my income.

MS. Do you find it easy or difficult to find friends down here?

ES. I find it difficult to find friends my age, which is fifty-fix. Most people my age are not retired yet, so they're not here. And the Mexican friends my age are such family people there aren't many common interests. I've been single for four years, and I'm not looking.

MS. Did you ever feel like you were really challenged here?

ES. When I first moved here, the contractor I had for this initial house ripped me off for forty thousand dollars. I hardly spoke any Spanish. The guy actually had talent but never intended to finish the job. He would bring people here to show off his work to get more contracts. He ripped everyone off. I wasn't here full-time yet. He and his workers were living in my house, and his kids were living here, too. All these people here. I came down with all my furniture, expecting to move into my house, and there was nowhere to land. I had to kick them out. He just left.

I had sent him money to pay workers and finish the project, and he never passed the money on to the subcontractors. There was no accountability with the money, no bank account. He did the same to others and probably walked with over one hundred thousand dollars. I went after him with the police and the help of a Mexican friend who had been ripped off by him, too, and who could speak the language and knew what was going on here better than I did. I was the only one with a written contract, so she wanted me to go after him.

He came after me with a lawyer, a lawsuit, and death threats. I had to get a lawyer and show up in court, but he never showed. To counter the death threat, I built the wall around my house, which still had no windows or doors. I moved to the room upstairs and put windows and doors in up there. There are cement stairs on the outside of the house leading to that room. I didn't put a handrailing on it so that it would be easier to push someone off if I had to. I slept with a breaker bar by my bed.

He even ripped off his wife's family, never giving them the money I had given him to pay for the *palapa* over the bus parked below. I had a bunch of people come to me saying the same thing. He never paid anyone the money I had given him to pay. My advice to people is to be on your land when you are building and go with people who have references. No matter if they Mexican or gringo, find out from other people what it was like to work with them. My other tip is don't hire someone who has a fancier car than yours!

My other challenge is feeling lonely, finding friendship. I ask myself, is it worth the loneliness to be here? The answer always comes up yes. If I were to sell this place with the beautiful ocean view and move up north, I could buy a little mold unit somewhere and still have to go back to work for a living.

MS. How much time do you spend on the computer?

ES. I don't have a computer. I have a device. I do e-mail and Facebook, and that's it. I don't Skype or call the States. I'd say fifteen, twenty minutes a day online.

MS. How was Hurricane Odile for you?

ES. The windows and doors blew off the upstairs rooms, so everything got shuffled. I was down in this room with the doors rattling. I moved furniture in front of them and tied them with dog leashes. I wired the window handles shut with hanger wires. Since then, I have put in sliding locks into the cement above and below to secure the doors.

The wires from the street poles were whipping across the roof tiles and breaking them all up. This house was wrapped in power lines in the morning. Water was coming in the brick wall in the kitchen like a cascade. The brick was dry when they laid it, and the mortar was too dry. So the mortar separated from the brick. In the *palapa* down below, the shower broke, so I lost all the stored water. It made the ground soggy, and the *palapa* tilted, ending up on the bus, and made holes in it. Compared to others, I was lucky and recovered in about a month.

MS. That was a whooper of a storm. I like hearing other people's accounts of it. Are you ever bored?

ES. No, never. I go camping, surfing, up to hot springs in the mountains. And if I get bored, I watch TV! I just got this one four months ago. First TV since I left home. I have Internet at my house and have Netflix. It's great. I've been catching up with media stuff that everyone else watches.

At this point in the interview, Elizabeth and I started on the Dream of the Future Tour, tripping through the construction zones. I absent-mindedly followed her into the bathroom connected to the room we were in. She washed her hands, and I looked around and saw a Japanese sitting tub. I had tried to make one at my house, but it never worked out proportion-wise. Hers had started life as a huge ceramic planter. She had drilled the drain hole and put it in place with the pipes to drain it and...voilá! She sanded it and put a sealing paint on it. I might have to try it; they conserve water, and that is always on my mind.

We went up the outside stairs to the bedroom, where the hurricane had blown through. She pointed out that the stairs now had a metal railing. She had been working here to add a kitchen, making it an apartment with a great view. Across a small outdoor patio was a separate bedroom attached to a spacious terrace with the panoramic Pacific view.

The next room in process was a little studio apartment to the left of the main house. On the ground were lots of bottles, which she explained were intended for a bottle wall she wanted to build herself. It would be cement and brick and bottles, which would let in light. She was a genius at repurposing *segunda* furniture for a new function. Here there was a unique chest being remade as a kitchen-counter and sink combination.

The new casita down the hill was also a studio apartment with more delightful, ingenious repurposing. In those small rooms, I could see the sea captain in her choices. She had created a small space with everything for efficiency and comfort and, I have to admit, the cutest little kitchens. But then again I like small.

The second story on the house in the lower corner was new. It used to have a *palapa* roof. Now with a second story built, it provided a view and a side terrace for outdoor living. The second story was the kitchen and living room space; downstairs had a bedroom and bathroom. All the rentals were provided with outdoor living space. People just do not spend all their time inside in this pleasant climate.

Elizabeth hoped to get $400 a month for the studio apartments and $600 a month for the room on top of her house with the kitchen and for the two-story house in the corner. Her place has a Facebook page called Casa Todas Amigas. Check it out. She said that pets are welcome if she knows beforehand.

She'd like to meet you. Call or come by!

Thanks, Elizabeth, for some great stories and a view of the future. *Bueno suerte* [good luck]!

CHAPTER 17

KAIA THOMSON

From my personal experience, I would describe Kaia as a California girl. It seems like they all have wide smiles and blond hair and are energetic, genuinely happy people. I imagine California must be a golden state. Here beside me was a person who was so happy with her life that she was bubbling over with the opportunity to share it. Kaia was bigger than me, with blue eyes and sunshine-induced rouge accenting her frequent smile. If I interrupted the text to insert how many times she laughed, guffawed, and said, "Wow," this interview would be too long to print. She often had a smile on her face when she was talking. Keep that in mind as you read this. Kaia suggested we go upstairs to the guest room because it was neater, not as many distractions. We sat at a big round table in the one-room apartment and commenced an interview which I knew had to be concise. Kaia was hard to pin down for a date and time because she was a busy woman with many time commitments due to her horses and classes she taught in horsemanship.

Kaia offered some early history of her times in Mexico. "My mother always had a great affiliation with Mexicans and Native Americans. One of my fondest memories is when I was four or five years old in the fifties, and we all would pile into the old Ford station wagon and drive to Tijuana to buy firecrackers. Mexico was not far from home. I was born in Hollywood and grew up playing around the Hollywood sign. We would put all the cherry bombs and Roman candles in the spare-tire well in the back and cover it with blankets. Then we kids would lie on it, sleeping, when we crossed the border back into the United States.

Mom loved Mexico and would cross the border often to purchase jewelry and textiles. We always had wonderful friends and neighbors from Mexico. I grew up loving Mexico. I am enamored with the Spanish language; it's beautiful, descriptive, and romantic and not as messed up as English. A word says what it means. "Sugar" can mean a lot of different things, but "*dulce*" means sweet.

MS. How did you come to live in Mexico later in your life? Here you have established yourself as a riding instructor, nature photographer, and naturalist writer.

Kaia Thomson (KT). I always had horses in my life, boarding and riding at Sunset Ranch, Hollywood Stables. I would put on little horse shows. We would ride on Friday nights over to Burbank to have dinner and ride back in the dark, a four-hour round trip. I worked in the old Horse Laundry. It was the only place in the San Fernando Valley that took saddle pads and blankets to wash and repair. There was a big horse area around Los Feliz Boulevard in Glendale. I had my horse boarded at another stable close by, and I learned classical dressage, jumping, and English-saddle-style riding.

MS. Were you the only one in your family who loved horses?

KT. Mom loved to ride. She rode this little horse named Chance. She'd always go riding with me. My mom died when I was twenty-four. My father left when I was four. Horses were my parents, so to speak. I had the best mom in the whole world. She gave me my sense of adventure. She was a professional artist, painting for her passion and painting for her work. She did fashion spreads for May

Company and Robinson's, for Bullocks and Catalina Swimwear. She painted album covers for Rosemary Clooney and Duke Ellington and others. She emigrated with her family when she was nineteen from Denmark and put herself through art school and then moved west to California.

Because of her Danish descent, I asked Kaia at this point if her hair was blond or white. She said that she was brunette and that now she called her hair "antique blond." She turned sixty-one this summer.

KT. I first came to Baja when the best horse of my career, after forty-five years of horses, somehow broke his foot in the corral and I had to put him down. I was so devastated that I was ready to give up horses for good. A friend asked if I wanted to go to Catalina Island for my birthday. I had been there once in forty-some years, and it's right across from Long Beach. I've always been a water baby, swimming, body surfing, and then I discovered scuba diving on that trip. I met my instructor and put on my gear. He helped me regulate my buoyancy, and we swam out to the buoy. The minute we descended, I was home. Oh my God! It was amazing. We swam all over that day. I got very involved with underwater photography and video. I learned to dive in California waters; it's cold water, lots of surge and wet suits. But the kelp is waving, and the sea life is amazing!

I came to La Paz to scuba dive on my fiftieth birthday. We went out with the Cortez Club. In the winter of 2004 to 2005, I came to Baja again to dive with friends at the Socorro Islands two hundred fifty miles south of Cabo. I had the thought then that "Maybe I want to bring some horses down and try living here." On May 18, 2005, we were diving in La Paz and it was too windy, so we decided to sight-see a little. I'd never done any exploring on my trips—just airport, hotel, dive, hotel, airport, bye!

We drove to La Ventana, and my thoughts were "This is the hottest, driest place I've ever been in my life! It's brown, and I don't see any horses." We decided to drive to Todos Santos. On the way, I'm noticing mountains, ocean, green plant life. It was feeling good. Always while flying from Cabo to LA, I would look down and wonder, what is that green place down there? Before when I have changed locations, the place has spoken to me. Todos Santos spoke to me. On December 5, 2005, I arrived in Todos Santos with horses and as much as I could fit in the trailer. *Menaje de casa* [*moving home*].

That was an adventure. I had never driven a mile in Mexico, and here I come with three horses in a giant truck and trailer. I learned that down here, you just go with the flow, and no matter what happens, it will work out. A Mexican friend, Alberto, drove down with me. At Guerrero Negro where you cross into Baja Sur, the guy at the inspection station says, "You can't cross because your papers say your destination is Tijuana." Alberto, bless his heart, got on a cattle truck with the papers and went all the way back to Tijuana.

I stayed at the inspection station for four days because, of course, it was a Friday. I had a grand time in Guerrero Negro. I stayed in a little hotel with a stash of Trader Joe's whole-wheat pasta and chocolate. At the inspection station where the horses were, they would unload cows and run them through the tick dip and then load them back on the trucks. These guys were running around in the dust after the cattle. I suggested we use my horses; they let me and my horses work the cattle. We had the funnest time. Alberto came back on Tuesday morning at one after visiting family in Tijuana and San Ysidro. So it worked out fine for everyone. We took off after he rested a bit and drove straight through, arriving in Todos Santos at eleven at night.

MS. Did you know Spanish at that time?

KT. I knew a lot of words but not tenses, and my conversation was atrocious. A little language story for you. My first riding friends in Todos Santos and I would ride around and visit people, feeling pretty special, like all newcomers do. People were so friendly, and they would play guitar for us and give us bags of chilies and offer us water. They asked us, "Who are you ladies?"

And we replied, "We're the *chicas calientes!*" [*hot chicks*] Of course we were all in our fifties. Then a friend one day says as he watches his dogs, "Ah, *mi pera es muy caliente.*" [My dog is in heat.] Realization: Oh, no, we've been riding all over town telling people we are the girls in heat! We had the biggest laugh. Here in the horse business, I have learned a lot of Spanish because often I am dealing with people who don't speak any English. It's an instant immersion class. Awesome!

MS. So here you are, arriving with three horses. Where did you go?

KT. I had horsey friends who had bought some land close to the beach north of Todos Santos. They already had corrals built. They had a casita for me to stay in, so the arrival was easy. We had four horses to begin with, and a few more arrived, as always. If you build it, they will come. Getting used to living here with horses was very different. I consider north of the border a consumer's paradise. It's not like that here. Back then, ten or twelve years earlier, things were really difficult. In terms of animals, here cows come first. They provide the meat, the milk, and hides for equipment and clothing. A horse is a commodity. There is no big money in the horse industry in Baja as there is on the mainland. It's challenging to get the medicines and supplies you need consistently. Now there are two good large-animal vets, one in La Paz and one in San Jose del Cabo.

Right away I had a new friend, Deborah, knocking at my door, wanting to learn how to ride. We rode all the time and became really good friends. Soon a little group of enthusiasts formed. Now I lease twenty acres on La Cachora Road and have twenty-three horses and a donkey. It's sort of like a cooperative of boarded horses: mine, others', some old ones just living out their lives, and some rescued ones. I am the manager, the one in the saddle holding the reins. It's fun to take kids to town on the horses and get a taco or ice cream. The local kids are excited. They say, "Oh. Your horses have shoes!"

The horses live a nomadic life in these parts. When it rains and there is grass, they are turned loose to eat, and they get fat. Then when it is dry and they are picking through the weeds, they get thin. My horses work, so they come first. They make money, and they get fed. We are very, very lucky, because for seven years, I have bought all our hay from a wonderful ranch, Rancho Chapingo, owned by Antonio Castillo, a professor of botany at Universidad al Chapingo. They put up a wonderful mix of grass and alfalfa, oat hay, oat and alfalfa mix, and all kinds of good stuff. I now know what time of year they will be putting up what, and they have a steady customer in me.

To do business here and not feel restricted, it is important to be legal, pay taxes, and have an accountant. When I went to do this at emigration, I was asked for my diploma validating my riding and teaching skills. What? I told them I was a writer and photographer, too, and they said, "Yeah. You and everybody else." It was hard then to get approval to make money here. I didn't have a diploma, so I dug out a lot of photographs and copied them on paper. I wrote in my best bad Spanish my mission statement, my whole life history of horses, and all the famous people I had taught to ride, like Sylvester Stallone. I laminated the cover and tied it up with ribbons; it was really cool. They accepted it with a grin and gave me permission. Now I have permanent-resident status and an accountant, so it is a little easier to build up the business.

MS. I have so appreciated the photographs and articles you have published in the *Todos Santos Journal del Pacifico* magazine. I can't imagine how you balance it all—the horses, the photography. and all the research you do for the magazine's wildlife articles.

KT. I've always loved taking pictures. I think I inherited my mother's artistic eye. I see shapes in rocks, colors in clouds. Photography is such a fantastic way to share the world. The digital world has brought so much beauty into people's lives. It's an amazing tool. I don't spend days waiting for a shot. More often the shot finds me. I'm walking and see something that takes my breath away. I go get my camera and click away. I frequently have my Nikon with its housing when I dive. Slowly I've built up an inventory.

I went to Pierce College in Woodland Hills, California, and had a couple years in Monterey studying natural-resources management, biology, and a little botany. I just took classes in what I wanted to learn, so I never got a degree. I have tons of identification books, plus the Internet for research. I am my own worst enemy when it comes to researching for an article, because I can access so much information that I never stop. One fact leads to another. They are all interesting, so I keep reading. I can turn a two-hour project into a twelve-hour project.

What I like about underwater photography is you don't choose your subjects; they choose you. You can follow a fish around and get a lot of fish-butt photos. But if you are interesting to a fish or a bird, it comes to you, and you get the sexy-face photos or an interaction. The natural world is very curious. It's hard to sneak up on a butterfly; if butterflies see movement, they're gone. There's a little game I play with, say, a bird. I'll get a distance shot, location. Then I take six steps and take another couple pictures. Then six steps again and again if they don't move. I try to Jedi knight my subjects: "Sit there, you will. Don't move, please."

MS. Have you had scary experiences out there taking wildlife pictures?

KT. No. I don't scare too easily. Some of my experiences could have totally freaked out and terrified other people. Once diving in California, I am propped up on my elbows waiting patiently for this goby fish to come out of his hole in the rock, and my legs with fins are stretched out behind me. I feel a little pull on the fin. I was all ready to get mad at a person swimming up on me. Underwater photographers dive alone so that others don't scare their subject or murk up the water.

But the tugging didn't stop. I turn around, and there is a harbor seal; they're the spotted ones. He smiles at me with his whiskers lifting up. I started talking to him: "You're such a cutie." He comes around and sits on my lap. We had a conversation about this and that, and I'm petting him. He swam with me back to the boat and let me hold his flipper and do circles and rolls together. [*Water ballet with a seal!*]

Another time, diving in some deep canyons in the Socorro Islands, I'm adjusting my camera for the light and have it aimed up when a shark's nose comes over the side of the reef above me. Stripes! A tiger shark! They kind of have a bad reputation. He goes on his way, but I felt so lucky to have had that visit. Our group then went up to about fifty feet, and the dive master signals, "Let's just drift." So we floated with the current as the boat followed along and watched the bubbles to pick us up.

We spotted a school of fish and drifted over into them. There were a couple hundred hammerhead sharks. I held my camera still and hardly breathed, because I didn't want a lot of bubbles to scare the sharks. They were schooling and sleeping. There, right close to me, were the gills, the teeth, the eyes, and the little cleaner fish. They were under me, beside me, over me. We just passed through them. It was an amazing, almost religious experience! I'm so used to being around large animals that big stuff doesn't scare me. Only once have I been really scared, up in Alaska, when on a hike, I hear a rustle in the bushes. I look over, and there are two bear cubs. I didn't know where the mother was and hoped I wasn't between her and her cubs. That was one of the few times that an animal has made my hair stand up. I just walked really fast and quietly out of there.

At that point in the interview with Kaia, I shared a few stories of animal encounters I had had, and then Kaia added, "The thing about horses and other animals is that they see things in black and white. People are so complicated, but to a horse, it is yes or no. They are wonderful role models.

"Our burro has recently taken up singing with the dogs. I call it the Doggy Donkey Opera. Pretty funny! Not many people have experienced a donkey braying right in their face. The burro's decibels are so strong it can be physically painful. They say you can hear a donkey fifty miles away. That's why they developed such big ears. It takes their full body, stomach muscles, and lungs heaving to bray like that.

"For sixteen years, I only rode mules. There are great mules and bad mules, and you can't change them. They are very dedicated to their person. I think that mules can truly reason, and that's why they don't panic. Horses will panic way faster than a mule. I've had mules save my life a couple times by refusing to cross a river. Self-preservation is strong in them. The locals here like a hinny, which is a donkey mother and a horse daddy. A mule is a horse mother and a donkey father. The hinny is a little hardier and can eat and fully digest palm leaves and cactus, as the donkey can. Pound for pound, a donkey is so strong."

MS. I once had a donkey in New Mexico. I called him Song and Dance. He certainly hauled a lot of stuff for me, even my two little boys. How many times a week do you go out riding with people?

KT. I ride almost every day. I ride for pleasure, and I ride for work. I have four horses that are special to me. I enjoy training them and doing upper-level work with them. I love riding them and teaching them things; I call it my Zen time. I love to ride. It's what makes me get up in the morning. I love to clean the corrals.

I love to feed. I love to care for everybody. I love to share this area on horseback. The horse just takes you there. You can look around and see stuff.

Occasionally I get people who have had a bad experience with a horse. I assure them that I will put a rope on their horse and stay close. Ninety-nine percent of the time, when we return, they are riding by themselves with a huge smile on their face because they did it! That's super wonderful to get someone over that hump in life. Horses are so therapeutic. They are so willing to share their energy. And I love sharing their energy with people. To ride through the huerta, a little bit of beach, and up into the desert, and the people are so grateful to have done that.

I don't have a nine o'clock, twelve o'clock, and thee o'clock. It's all by reservation. There's an ad in the *Journal*, and I work with the eco-adventure groups who also advertise in the *Journal*. It's expensive to keep the horses, so it's not that lucrative. When everyone is here in the high season, we probably teach twenty-five lessons a week with the kids. In the summer, it's ten or twelve lessons a week. We have two special-needs kids who come and ride, and a couple more from town.

I wish we had a person here who is trained in equine-assisted therapy. I know a little, but I'm not qualified really. The kids aren't severely disabled. We work on pronunciation, motor skills, grooming, riding. Maybe someday someone with that skill will come. That's one thing I like about here. You get an idea and project it to the gods, and needs tend to manifest quickly. It is pure here, not much pavement, lights, air traffic, noise, negative energy. So when you concentrate, your message is sent directly to your helpers.

MS. I've noticed that same thing here. Do you have challenges down here?

KT. The trickle effect from Odile was that the food sources got destroyed. My supplier lost their transformer and had to replace it themselves, which took time, so they couldn't irrigate to grow the crops. I got by with stored hay for six weeks, then expensive nasty stuff, and then grass and rabbit pellets. By April, we could resume normal feeding, but it was seven months of improvising.

Another challenge for foreigners is to not make assumptions about being understood or that you understood what your Mexican helper said. Get specific; clarify. You never stop learning down here, which is one thing I love about it. Stop agonizing about the things that go wrong. Things usually work themselves out. Learn patience, and have faith. Your worry is not going to change things. Stop doing that to yourself.

We had a couple of big fires in the huerta a couple years back. One headed right for the horses. The palm trees were blowing their tops because all their debris hanging down on them was burning and heating up the water stored within them, and then their tops explode. Pretty dramatic! The pump in town was broken, so we had no water to hose down the area. What to do? *Mi comadre* [female friend] Euva asked me, "What is your spirit telling you right now?" I said, "Things are going to be fine." Just then a backhoe showed up and started creating a firebreak and saved the day.

When Odile hit us in the middle of the night, I thought, "God showed up!" The noise of the solar-panel cables stretching and breaking, roofs flying by and piling up on the side of the house, and trees groaning was tremendous. By four in the morning, I was tired of mopping up water. In the morning, we couldn't drive to the horses because of all the poles, wires, and trees lying across the roads. So we walked, climbing over everything to get to the horses. The horses had not one scratch and were hungry and expecting breakfast as usual. The CFE [*electric company*] needs to be commended for their quick response. I had power back in eleven days.

Kaia and I descended to ground level which she called her "green cave" because of all the trees and plantings you could see out of the windows. The first floor looked like the house of a busy person whose life was lived outside for the most part. In the open design was a large, well-used easel she had bought from an artist friend. Resting on it was a floral painting by Kaia's mother and three framed paintings of landscapes with horses. They were waiting to be hung.

She hadn't mentioned buying or building so I asked her if she owned or rented.

Kaia said, "I have rented here for 10 years. My landlady is a fantastic gal who lives in the States."

MS. Do you feel like you have integrated into the Mexican culture much?

KT. Yes, because of the horses. Almost everyone has a horse. It's a rancho culture, and a horse is transportation. I'm still here doing this, and it is satisfying to be a part of the community with the horses. Most of the people I am in regular contact with are very happy. It's admirable how they take care of their family members.

Here if you're not quite right, if you're gay, nobody cares. If you have spinach in your teeth, nobody tells you. I had an old five-tiered skirt with ribbons at the tiers, and I had been wearing it around town all day, shopping, paying bills, visiting friends, and so on. When I got home and looked in the mirror, where I had been sitting was shredded. The ribbons had held the skirt together, but the fabric had just given up. I had been to the water company with all the men sitting there and the bank, all the places you go. No one told me. Somehow there is a beauty about it.

MS. I find the Mexican people extremely polite. They wouldn't tell you about your ripped skirt, just like they won't correct your Spanish unless they know you really well. Sounds like you are busy each day from start to finish.

KT. Well, yeah. Horses are a lifestyle. One cannot put them in the garage and then get them out and then put them back in.

There is a lot of responsibility, for sure. And then there is writing the book, perhaps. How about *Memoires of a Hollywood Cowgirl*?

MS. I look forward to reading that one. Have you learned anything important about yourself living here?

KT. Yes. When I moved down here, it was a big thing to do. You can feel a little too proud of yourself. You feel a little larger than life. "Wow, I drove all this stuff down, and I'm going to do all these things." Then in a few years' time, you figure out that life is a whole lot larger than you. When the plumber doesn't show up, there is more going on than just you. He took his mother to the hospital, his uncle from Tijuana just showed up, or it's his son's birthday party.

My brother said, and I agree with him, "A place like this will, for many reasons, completely tear you apart, but it also puts you back together better than you were before." My friends in the States asked me why I would want to move to Mexico. They said, "You have everything here that you want." My answer was, "Why not?" The rockiest roads lead to the most beautiful places. It gets rocky now and again, but then the next day dawns with a pink and orange sunrise.

MS. I can see by the sun that it is time for you to go feed. I thank you for spending some time with me. I always wanted to talk to a wildlife photographer. You've contributed so much to everyone's knowledge of this place that we foreigners now call home. Thanks for training the horses and keeping them healthy so that some of us can see and feel the landscape so intimately. It's a worthy endeavor: knowing the ecosystem we call home.

CHAPTER 18

NANETTE HAYLES

I arrived at the appointed hour for the interview with Nanette, but no one was home. A workman said he had seen her downtown and would call and let her know I was here. I decided to walk around the grounds and check things out while I waited. Earlier that week I had lost my mobile phone, and my son had come for an unexpected, week-long visit. I was so contented to talk to him that I never needed to use the phone. All this to say, I should have called first to remind her of our date, which we had set three weeks earlier, but I had no phone.

I had been to the house twice before. Once for a Vepasana Buddhist, all-day, silent meditation retreat and once for an art showing of Nanette and her daughter's art. The name of the show was Synergy. Her land was a few acres in all, at the edge of town, butting up against a hill that separated Todos Santos from the beach. I noticed right away a ten-by-twelve-foot bed of yarrow, all ferny and softly green. Next to it was a raised, tiled fountain, five feet by five feet, with a tiled Guadalupe mural on the back. It had its own shade roof made of palm fronds. The water in it was light green with feathery green towers and knolls. I thought that I saw tadpoles and little fish.

I wandered to the entrance patio, where there was a table draped in a colorful Mexican oilcloth. It was same pattern as mine at home. I'll bet she bought it at the old Casa Tota tienda, where I bought mine. Shading this was a ramada-style *sombra* [shade]: sticks of *palo d'arco* laid down tightly across beams and posts of mauto and other mountain hard woods. It was very rancho, giving me appreciation for the Mexicans' simple solutions that don't need a trip to town for nails.

The shade was sheltering orchids, begonias, other shade-loving plants in pots and, of course chairs for waiting. Within sight was an adobe building with wide doors, which I knew was a gallery for art showings. Butted up against it was an area that was Nanette's studio, but now it looked like it was another kind of workshop. Turns out, she gave it to her son-in-law when her daughter and he came to join her in Baja Sur.

The entrance patio to the adobe house was filled with art, both sculptural and flat. My favorite one was a meter square board, painted blue, with a landscape of tin scrapes depicting the sea, mountains, palms in the wind, and a sun with its rays of nails projecting outward. To the right was a blue metal gate leading into an area shaded by tall coco palms and even taller Washingtonian fan palms, a hardy endemic palm of Baja.

This was home to a large, fenced chicken yard with a big, white rooster strutting around talking rooster to me. I learned later that the chickens were in the henhouse, avoiding the new rooster. This was only his second day here. In the corner of the patio, behind doors made of woven *palo d'arco* sticks, was an outdoor bathroom with toilet and shower, such a convenient feature for workers and trips to the garden.

A side patio was protected by a lofty dormer, which jutted out from the L-shaped house, causing an elegant, high *palapa* roof over a patio of a hundred uses, such as bicycles, blue water-storage barrels, a long comfy couch, and a long, rustic table covered in a purple Guatemalan cloth with sparkling threads and graced with a vase decked out in seashells. From the high rafters clung a dozen hornet nests, all empty now, awaiting another warm season. Next to the patio was a barbecue grill of rancho proportions set in a raised, tiled prep table. I'll bet many a good meal was cooked there.

To the right was another gate leading to an area of groomed and irrigated herb and vegetable beds, shaded by *maya sombra* [shade cloth]. All the beds were surrounded by cement blocks or stones, the irrigation ditches lined with cemented rock, and the whole area was bordered by beautiful rock walls. I could tell this area was old because the fruit trees were big and battered, probably from Hurricane Odile of 2014. I spotted a shrine to the Mother Goddess made of block and topped with a flat stone. Inside was a bust of herself waiting for you to sit on the stone bench opposite, which was planted around with roses, and pay her some due respect.

I wandered down to another level and spied an old corral made of *palo zorillo* posts—a favorite for posts because its hardwood nature goes on and on without rotting. It has a wonderful twisted growth pattern that I always enjoy seeing when it is used. They kept horses here when the children were growing up, I was told later. In front of me were big, empty areas that look freshly scraped. I learned later that there were years when these were leased to a friend who planted them in sage and mint, but now they were the mass graves of cleanup from the hurricane. On this same yard level, I discover a twenty-two-foot-diameter circle made with the pink stones you see north of La Paz. Holding down the center was a log stump with a white rock on it. Sacred ground, no doubt, to inspire reverence for the circle of life. On the other side of the house was another rock circle, a tribute to the sun; the former, I learned later, was a tribute to the moon.

I saw two shallow birdbaths while I was walking. I wish I had one.

Just as I returned to the entrance porch, in walked the *dueña*, Nanette Hayles. She was sorry for being late, but she said that she hadn't eaten much in the last two days and had taken herself out to breakfast. She was wearing midcalf, earthy-colored, comfortable pants and a thin, cotton-print shirt, perfect for the growing heat of early July. She unlocked the door, which was protected by a deep, recessed, handmade adobe arch and walls, with prayer flags fluttering. The handmade wooden door had a carving of clasped hands, like in a handshake, surrounded by a carved oval in a twisted rope design. She stepped inside gesturing with a sweeping arm, and speaking softly, said *"Pasale"* [literally: pass over it, meaning: come in]

Inside, my eyes were drawn to the gleaming white and Caribbean-blue, tiled floor laid in a diamond, checkered pattern. The room was one big circle, maybe thirty feet in diameter, with everything included—an oval, pueblo-style fireplace on one wall, a round table for eating, a long kitchen island, and a long table laid out with art supplies and more. I couldn't notice everything at once, but I did notice the arched doorway, which led out of the circular room and down a tiled corridor, presumably to the bedrooms.

I asked if I could see this wing. It had a big office and two spacious bedrooms, looking even more grand because of the high *palapa* roof overhead. Nanette told me that the *palapa* roof was over twenty years old and would soon be replaced with tin. The door opening off to the right was her bedroom suite, with its own walled courtyard and huge bathroom. One day it would be sectioned off from the rest of the house and rented as an apartment for artists who need a place to live. She said that many artists have stayed in her house in the past, along with family members.

The past started in 1990, when she and her husband came to Todos Santos and bought the land and unfinished house. Nanette said, "There were no floors, windows, or kitchen and very crude, raw, unfinished cement. There was a toilet in the bathroom, but the shower was a meter-deep pit with slated boards over it. It was scary, because scorpions, centipedes, and cockroaches were climbing around in there. I would rather hose off in the yard. There were no homes out here then. It was you and nature living together. No screens. There was a roof for rain and walls, and that's about it. Nothing to keep nature out. We had frogs, feral cats, and bats in the house every night."

It was a beautiful, spacious house and I was curious to get the whole story. We returned to the round table in the round room and began the interview.

MS. Had you been to Todos Santos before?

Nanette Hayles (NH). Patrick, my husband, is a finished carpenter, making fancy kitchen units and entertainment centers for homes in Brentwood and Bel Air in the west LA area. He was really stressed at the time. One of the designers said he had a place in Cabo San Lucas and said, "Take your wife and go. Here are the keys, but you have to go to see Todos Santos." We rented a car to drive to La Paz, and Todos Santos was on the way.

I was blown away by the incredible sense of peace I felt in this tiny town. We got in touch with a realtor who is still my friend, Kathy Buchanan, who came to the area in the eighties. We agreed to meet her on our way back to Cabo and see available places. We continued on to La Paz, where my ex stopped in front of the church and said, "Get out and meditate and see what we're supposed to do."

So I meditated and asked for guidance. We spent the night in a cute little hotel that had a monkey. When we went back to Todos Santos, Kathy wanted to show us a house. "We only want to see historical buildings," said Patrick. So we saw them, but I encouraged Patrick to go see the house Kathy had in mind. When we walked through the gate, a big, booming voice said, "You're supposed to be here." I had never received quick guidance like that before! The house was unfinished, and Patrick was inspired to finish it. So he wrote Kathy a check to hold the house. I was blown away! That was quick; was it for real?

We cut our vacation short and went back to LA in early June. Patrick encouraged me to go see my friend Brother Turiyananda, a monk at the Self-Realization Fellowship. He was my best friend and mentor for twenty years. He had foreseen many things that would happen in the world: people losing their homes, economic collapse, and so on. He very plainly said, "Leave! Start over again down there." He predicted a time when the whole planet would be stressed and tested.

I'm telling you this story because it has affected my whole life. He then told me his time is up: "I have permission. I can go now. I am free." He was a robust man in his sixties. He said, "Don't worry. I'll be there to help from the other side. I'll help you move and everything." That was on a Thursday, and on Sunday morning, I got word that he had passed. I was deeply stunned and saddened.

We put our house up for sale, and it sold right away. Patrick also sold his business right away. That was in 1990, when one of the first economic crises happened. By the fifteenth of September, we were here in Mexico. We sold everything, closed our lives up north, imported everything, did the emigration thing, and started our new lives. There were only two other families here in our neighborhood with children our kids' age. The town then was about ninety-nine-point-nine percent Mexicano. It was such an adventure! My kids were eight, two and a half, and almost a year.

MS. My goodness! You were a mother of young children when you took this on. That takes strength and determination. Did you leave a career behind in LA?

NH. Yes, I taught gifted children in Oakland for about a year and then in Los Angeles for many years, at the primary school level. I have a postgraduate degree from UC Berkeley in education and was part of an experimental school where alternative methods were taught and practiced. I witnessed *real* learning and was especially impressed by the selection of teachers. Teachers were hired based solely on their ability to reach and teach children, not on their personal self-expression. The school was situated in the worst area of Oakland, where race, socioeconomic background, and other social "disadvantages" were prominent.

However, all these variables had less and less effect when it came to a child learning. The environment was safe, encouraging, and friendly, and the teachers loved teaching! These ingredients made the child motivated. The children wanted to know things; they wanted to learn, and they retained what they learned. Also the curriculum was *smart* and challenging, involved problem solving, and engaged the students in finding and discovering answers. This is the career I left, but I carry it with me and try to practice what I learned way back then.

Nanette's description of alternative education reminded me of a book I read when I had young children called *Education Is Ecstasy*. Here was a woman of my own heart and hope for the human race. This beautiful woman in front of me was mixed blood by a Jamaican father, which is, by and large, a mixture of black, East Indian, and British. Her eyes were brown, big, and alive and were set in an oval, well-proportioned face with a few small freckles dancing across her nose and cheeks. Silvery-white, gray, and black hair with body and natural waves and curls framed her expressive face. She told me that she had recently stopped dying it. Her body had the natural fullness of a curvy, soft woman in her mid-sixties.

MS. Did you know Spanish when you came down?

NH. Some. That was the language I taught in a bilingual classroom; it was primarily a Latin American and Afro American student body. Patrick was so fluent in Spanish that the Mexicans thought it was his first language.

MS. That is a good way to begin down here. Not all people who come here speak Spanish when they arrive. So he must have brought down all his tools.

NH. We shipped everything down on a forty-foot truck. Half household and half tools, with all the papers signed and sealed. Everything was done legally. We got FM3 emigration status and did all the paper work by ourselves, never hired anyone to help us.

MS. What happened to the husband?

NH. In 1996 or 1997, we split company. There's something about Todos Santos that makes you go within, and then you have to adjust. I think it was an inside-evolution thing. When that happens, some of the glue that holds a marriage together just falls by the wayside. The stress of building and all the outside stuff can spiral people closer together or spin them apart. On a personal level, we all pick our own time to go to the next step. I had constant contact with my monk-friend-mentor for twenty years. That kind of person molds your life. My life was infused with that spirituality.

Patrick and I were on two different tracks. We had different ideas about raising our kids and other things. I was more dedicated to my spiritual life, and he leaned on me for that instead of doing his own spiritual work. When you live a spiritual life, it is more than just words. I couldn't do it for us anymore. I had to do it for myself. He still lives here in Todos Santos and has his design and construction business. His name is Patrick Coffman, if anyone wants his services. We are good friends and have a happy family. Life is too short.

MS. How were your kids educated?

NH. One went through the whole system here. Another finished high school and college in the United States, and one went to a good prep high school in La Paz and continued on to do two years of architecture school in Mexico. My daughter now lives here with my grandchild. My oldest son uses this place as a base and travels all over the world. He is an energetic healer and works with a group of people from all around the world. I didn't believe in it at first, or my son, the "healer," and now I'm blown away by it.

This was about the third time in the interview that Nanette had been "blown away" by the plot shifts in her own consciousness. I think she liked those moments of opening to amazement and growth!

MS. When did you get into art here?

NH. I've always been into art. When I was a child living at home and making art, my parents said, "Remember, you have to get a real job, too." I always made art even while I was teaching for sixteen years: paper tile, drawing, pen and ink, painting in different mediums. I do more now than I did then.

In the mid-1990s here, there was a small group of artists who got together to talk and share. We would meet at the Todos Santos Cafe; it was a fomenting group of inspiration and support. It was probably my favorite time here. Michael Cope, Derrell and Walker Buckner, Robert Whiting, Charles Stewart, Gloria Van Jansky, and I would paint together, play volleyball together, have brunch together. Some days we would paint and work all day. After all, we had to fill Michael Cope's new gallery! It lasted about ten years, and it is now a sweet memory. I knew Gabo then, too, who is world renowned; he would travel and bring artists back from Spain and Mexico City. There was a small group of Mexican artists here, too.

Then different types of people came as the amenities picked up. The first wave were pioneers. Then Fernando Salas invested here; his family built one of the first big hotels in Cabo. He is one of Mexico's prominent economists who helped write the NAFTA agreement. People thought he was an outsider, but he is a Mexican in his own country and had been visiting the Baja since he was a child.

It's a shame that more *estranjeros* don't integrate with the Mexicanos. I got to do that. I remember in the early 2000s when

Salas called me up and said, "I have all these guests [*various Latin American economists, one from Spain, and federal representatives of INAH*], and my chef had an emergency and can't come. What am I going to do?" I told him to bring them here! They came loaded with all kinds of fresh fish and vegetables. I put everyone to work. We chopped and prepped; we poured wine and tequila, set the table together. My kids were helping, mingling, sitting, being.

The leading economist from Spain spoke the most beautiful Spanish I have ever heard; his voice tone and everything, it sounded like music. I was too embarrassed to speak Spanish with him. He said, "That's all right; we can speak in English." All of them could speak two, three, four languages, and during the evening, the language of the conversation would change. Someone would say something in French, and they would all change to French. I was happy to see my kids and Dr. Salas and his friends all enjoying themselves. It was another magical moment that made my house a home.

There were times when I would just sit with some of the older people of the town who knew so much, and they told us about the abundance in the ocean, the turtles all coming up to nest. They were so smart! And most of them had third or fourth grade educations. I was shocked by how worldly they were. They just knew things by vibrations. They just knew stuff from being in touch with nature. It taught me a lesson in not being prejudiced and judging people by how simple their lives were, dirt floors and water barrels. Some of them are among the most wise, incredible people I have ever met. They had the ability to just experience joy! They are so in the moment, sharing their lives with one another. They taught me; I learned how to be here.

MS. How would you describe Todos Santos now?

NH. I feel like it is just like the rest of the world. There are people who try to create unity. I'm totally impressed with the Palapa Society, which represents unity and working together. I bow in respect to that group. They include the opinions, values, and beliefs of the Mexicans. In that organization, both gringo and Mexicano are on the same path of the heart. Even language is not a barrier. There are interpreters to help. I would like to see that with the artists.

There used to be the same unity in our early art festivals, which were incredible. People came from everywhere…no parking spaces! Who really started those festivals was Alice Corado of El Molina Trailer Park. They had it there for years. It grew and became too political. Everyone wanted to be the leader. I remember Gabo told me, "Watch out! Politics kill the spirit of art." I asked Gabo how we could prevent this from happening to the Latino Film Festival, brought to us by Silvia Perel and her late husband Leonardo. He said to go to the Institute de Cultura de Anthropologia y Historia and see if the film festival could become a part of it. Under that umbrella, it would have a life. [The *Institute de Cultura de Anthropologia y Historia (INAN) is an arm of the federal government established to promote the preservation of the national culture and historic sites.*]

Nanette and I spent a few minutes sharing our feelings of gratitude for the film festival that had grown so big, along with Youth in Video, the film school for the children of the town. The film they made two years ago and premiered at the festival was a silent film about the sugar-cane industry of old in Todos Santos. There were local adults in starring roles, and I noticed a greater attendance of Mexicans in the audience. They came to see their friends and relatives in the movies! The two of us have learned so much about Mexico and the whole Spanish-speaking world through the films at the festival. It's very successful for the town and the region and is now a part of the Institute de Cultural.

Nanette then said, "Some of the gringos who come to the area love Mexico, but without the Mexicans. They want to cut and paste what they knew there onto here. I see more of that here than I saw before. We have the extremes and everything in between. As the planet shifts and changes, it is demanding that we make decisions. Everything is changing. We either adopt unity, or we maintain our separateness.

"But people have to choose their time of change. We have to be patient with our friends and family and communities. It's taken me a long time to learn that, and I'm still learning. Do I, myself, really see God in every eye? We have to be rid of the conflicting beliefs within us. You can't claim Jesus if you have hate in your life. We have to get to know our inner selves and develop our skills, and then we can influence others. Start with self, and then as parents, we can influence our children. Then that child influences his or her circle of friends. It is the ripple effect in action."

MS. How do you finance your life here?

NH. Teaching classes, artwork. I try to provide art for every economic level with cards, posters, low-cost prints, high-end prints, and originals. I want people at any level to have art; I want to make it affordable. I'm not doing it just for me; I do it because art is important. Some kids never have a little piece of art.

You want to know how I live? Here is how I live. I changed my concept of God, the first source. Like some churches, I had believed that God was conditional, judgmental, mean, punishing. Now I refuse to believe that. I now believe that I am a child of God, the first source. And I believe everybody else is, too. Miracles have always happened in my life! Like finding this house, having that monk friend, my kids, and many other blessings. I am learning that we are taken care of by the cosmos, but we are afraid to believe that. Now every time I worry, I relax, I meditate, and I *let* life happen. Everything I need will come to my door. I believe that God is love and that abundance means having what you need when you need it.

And since I have been relaxing inside and trusting and I have changed my idea of what God is, I am happier. I judge less. I am more authentic, and when I meditate, I meditate with more intention; I am more focused. I feel the sacredness of it. I am opening up this communication where I can actually feel the presence. It's not words anymore. It's not a concept. It's an experience. I feel it so much that I want to cry out with joy. I can feel the subtle layers.

MS. Have you ever had challenges down here?

NH. Hell, yes, and who doesn't? One of the scariest but most heartwarming was when I thought I had to leave Mexico because of my divorce. Evidently back then, being a single woman with three kids put me in another category. I went back to the emigration office numerous times to renew my papers, but I felt a block. Finally I approached the head official and asked him point-blank what the problem was. He said frankly that he had never had a situation like mine and didn't know what to do. I asked him what would make it easier for him. His reply was to bring in my ex-husband.

I did, and while sitting there, I began to cry, realizing how much I loved living in Todos Santos. Patrick assured him that he was remaining in Todos Santos and would *not* abandon his family, me or his kids, and that I was also working as an artist. The emigration officer was still nervous, and after about an hour more of waiting and tears streaming down my face, he said, "Hay, yah, yah, OK!" And his hands slapped the desktop. I cried harder, and we all signed more papers. We all hugged each other. "*Bienvenidos* [welcome]," he said with a twinkle in his eye.

Another challenge I had—have—is living in an intolerable world. I think we *all* face this challenge, some more than others. The ripple effects keep coming toward us, and we keep sending it outwards. Our ability to be compassionate is waning. We, as a group, as a collective, don't see that everything starts here inside, within each of us. We don't practice compassion because we haven't learned to be compassionate with our own selves, our own bodies, our own minds.

To make things worse, we don't ever acknowledge ourselves as spirits. We still think of ourselves as human beings having some spiritual experiences, when actually we are spirits experiencing life as humans. When will we stop and listen and hear and be kind to ourselves, to each other, and to our planet? We cannot do this until we see ourselves as spirits residing in bodies that happen to have brains, even if we barely ever use them. All other challenges do not exist for me anymore. Compassion is the one I am working on.

MS. That is a good one to work on. I find I am more compassionate when I know more about the person and his or her circumstances. How do you get the news? Any kind of news.

NH. I go on the Internet, and I am guided to find all kinds of information. Interestingly I have discovered that scientists are breaking away from universities and corporate-sponsored programs and are going out on their own and sharing on the Internet. This is happening more and more. You can read about anything. You can learn about anything online. I go through phases as to how much time I spend online. For that art piece over there, I have spent hours researching online. That piece is called *Heal Thyself.* I learned about the kabbalah, the phi ratio, the Fibonacci sequence, the way the brain works.

As Nanette was speaking, I got up and went over to a table, where a four-by-eight-foot piece of plywood was laid out with a drawing of a life-size man with chakras illuminated and symbols in the margins.

NH. I go back and forth working on this project and others. This project represents two or three years of research. I don't try to create it. I ask for guidance. I ask myself, "What do you want on here?" It started out with organs and glands and which chakras they are related to, including the colors that represent them. Then they said to illustrate the brain. Then they said to do the heart. The heart was the hardest. The secret of the heart is the valves, working in two vortices and eight layers of muscles, in coordination with the other valves, pushing and pulling the blood through the heart. The heart is geometry in motion. It is a cube and a triangle. They move within each other. We try to make everything solid and stationary, but the heart is in constant geometric motion. I have discovered it is the Holy Grail!

This has been the only artwork where I was told what to do in lucid dreaming. I don't even take credit for it. It took months, step by step. It was an incredible experience to work on this.

Nanette then pointed out the details of the symbols and design. It was too much to write down, but maybe we'll all have an opportunity to see the work finished and Nanette speaking about the meanings she was guided to include. It was a beautiful teaching tool, incorporating many disciplines and interpretations of how we work as humans—body, mind, and spirit.

NH. Simultaneously I have been writing a bilingual children's book on meditation. I have never worked on two projects for so long. Why? In my lucid state, I was told that until I live and experience what I have created, the work will not be impregnated with love and wisdom, which will heal others. If I incorporate it into my life, then that knowledge will come out to the viewer or reader. Writing this book brought my meditation practice to another level. There is more integrity and intention now, a true union with God, the first source.

I am becoming more aware. To create a work called *Heal Thyself,* well, I have to do that, too. So I have been. My hand broke, and I never went to a doctor. I've been healing it for three years, and it is getting better. I also had a knee problem where my knee would give out. It is healed now. So I've been applying what I have learned in the research. My posture is better. I stopped dying my hair, and I cut down on drinking alcohol. My heart rate is slower, which means I am resting inside more. I am experiencing healing myself, so I believe what I have been learning. People will be more inclined to believe when they see the work or read the book because someone, myself, has lived it. It's no longer just a concept.

If you want to read about Nanette's book, *Wow of the Heart/Guau del Corazon,* go to www.nehayles.com/book. The first part of the book is a story of a boy, Matisse, and a bird, See More, and the way that they learn to meditate in a fun way and learn the ways of the heart. The second part is a guide for adults and children, encouraging and providing themes for self-inquiry, group discussion, and active participation. It is a book of practice in self-learning. On the website, there are also photos of Nanette's artworks. If you don't know what paper mosaic is, you can see it online.

MS. How did Hurricane Odile affect you?

NH. If you could see my huerta before, it looked so much more lush and had many more trees. It took me a year to pile up three mountains of debris. I just got rid of the last mountain last week [*one and three-quarter years later*], thanks to a friend and his truck. I had a bulldozer move those mountains. I also lost four eighty-year-old mango trees. The stress of the event killed a lot of plants.

My daughter, who was nine months pregnant, and her husband and I were in the closet that whole night when Odile came. It was very quiet in there. I did a piece of artwork dedicated to the event. The lesson was unity, as I watched Todos Santos come together; we supported and helped one another with love and kindness, something we should all keep in mind when climate change challenges our community. Mom-and-pop stores could go buy in La Paz , stock their little stores and extend credit to their neighbors, so no one went without food. The ejido had wells, so we had water. People are still recuperating, still stepping over logs in their front yards.

MS. Do you have plans for the future? Are you going to go back to the States?

NH. My future is to continue studying and researching how to combine art, science, and spiritual evolution. How do I, we, go from selfish to selfless? How do we transmute and transcend our identities—get beyond race, the job, religion, gender, and so on—and see what it is that makes us all the same? For me, through meditation, there is a synchronicity that evolves within the body and the mind, where the spirit gets to emerge and manifest itself. This is our bond; all of us are tiny sparks of God, spirit, first source. This is what I dedicate myself to finding out. So far I'm beginning to see it is actually the only part of our self that is real. Everything else is borrowed and has an expiration date. And, yes, I will go back and visit my wonderful brothers and friends in the States.

MS. Sounds good! I look forward to all your artworks to come. Thanks for sharing so deeply from your heart. I know it is your intent to help the world find greater love and understanding.

CHAPTER 19

DEBORAH STEPHENS

The house that Deborah Stephens was caretaking was one I had been in before. It was unique, in that it was built into a hill, so half of it was in the ground. It had a cement roof covered with dirt, which seemed like it would be cooling for this climate. It was the home of an architect wife and contractor husband, who raised two children there and built other beautiful homes in the same neighborhood, Las Tunas, about two miles up the coast from Todos Santos. After many years in it, they built another, bigger house, sold this one, and moved. The new owners changed the interiors to slick, modern, gray concrete. But it was still beautiful. Deborah was there until November, and then it would be an Airbnb rental.

We sat outside on a shaded patio, which captured a lovely breeze from the ocean not far away. I learned that Deborah had come to live in Todos Santos just over a year ago, but she was no stranger to the Baja peninsula. In 1983, she had visited a friend who had bought a bar in Cabo San Lucas and had told her how beautiful it was.

Deborah said, "I didn't come again until 1993. I was living in San Diego and started exploring Baja with some adventurers

179

who had traveled the Baja many times. One was Norman Roberts, who wrote *The Baja Plant and Field Guide*; another was Graham Mackintosh, who wrote *Into a Desert Place.* He's an Englishman who walked the perimeter of Baja. It took him about three years."

MS. How did you meet these incredible people?

Deborah Stephens (DS). I joined the Discover Baja Adventure Club in San Diego. I'm still a member. The first thing I did was sign up for a tour of the Guadalupe Valley with Graham Mackintosh. He didn't know that the date he had chosen for the tour was Super Bowl Sunday, so no one showed up but me. I got a private tour! He said, "You love Baja so much that I want to introduce to my friends so that you can keep exploring." He introduced me to Marvin and Aletha Patchen, Harry Crosby, Eve Ewing, Trudi Angell, and many more: a loose group of explorers who had been exploring the Baja for twenty-plus years. Bush pilots and the sort. They took me under their wing, and I hung out with them for several years.

MS. That is quite the beginning for a Baja peninsula love affair. Where did you come from? City? Country? Were you a career person in the States? What did you do?

DS. I was a human-resource director for a start-up biotech company in Seattle, which was bought by Bristol-Myers Squibb. I did the same for start-up companies in San Diego and had my own company there recruiting scientists for other companies. I had just spent ten years working sixty hours a week and attending night classes, obtaining two degrees: an undergraduate and a master's in business. I was in my mid-thirties before I even went to college. I was so burned out; I wanted to do something for myself. The plan was that when my divorce was final, I would take a year off and move to La Paz to study and do something just for me, which I had never done. There was no relaxation for me in ten years.

MS. So while waiting for one chapter to end, you would cross into Mexico and explore Baja. Nice. What did you like about it?

DS. I'm a nature person, so I loved the birds and plants that are different and getting away from the city. One of the first trips I took with the group was camping in some of the east-side canyons, above Laguna Salada, in the northern part of Baja. While we were hiking, we found a cave with an ancient bow and some arrows in it. We left them there and told the museum in Ensenada about them. They asked if we would go back and carefully wrap them up and bring them back, which we did. They made an exhibit in the museum around them. Things like that are thrilling, and that can happen in the Baja.

After San Diego, I lived in southern Africa for three years. In northern Botswana, I worked in a hospital as a human-resource person solving all sorts of people problems. When I got back, I moved to Santa Fe and worked part-time. I lived there eight years before coming here. I knew I could never go back to corporate life.

When I got back from Africa, I had friends asking me if I would take them to Africa and the Baja. So for the last fifteen years, I have taken people to see the whales at San Ignacio and the cave paintings in Sierra San Francisco, to Copper Canyon, and to Botswana. It was all just word-of-mouth, and it was only one or two trips a year. It all started with a friend in San Diego who had never been camping and who asked if I would take her into the Baja. So for two weeks, we drove and camped our way to Loreto and saw the whales in the San Ignacio Lagoon. When I came back to Baja after the long absence, I realized how much I missed it. I always wanted to spend more time here. In 2015, Trudi Angell asked me if I would house-sit for her for a month in Loreto. And I haven't been back to the States since.

MS. How and when did you get to Todos Santos?

DS. The first time was in 1995. The day my divorce was final, I drove to La Paz and lived there for a year. I was in my early forties at the time. It was a little hard being a single woman alone then.

I wanted to study Spanish, but there were not many classes except at the university in La Paz. I felt like I didn't even know enough to sign up for the class, so I didn't. I just studied my books at home and then would go out in the streets and try to speak.

Deborah was now sixty-four. She was slim and trim and in shape, with short, blond hair and black eyeliner, which made it so that I never noticed the color of her eyes. She wore her sunglasses almost the whole time because we were outside. She spoke with a soft, clear voice and gave the impression that she didn't get rattled easily. A good trait for one who took greenhorns out into the Baja wilderness.

DS. I couldn't understand why people I knew had been so positive about Todos Santos, because what I saw was a dusty, little town. So I thought I would stay a night. I ran into Robert Whiting, who was just then renovating the Todos Santos Inn. I rented the one room he had available. The town was quiet and had character, and there was a quality to the light.

MS. So you house-sat in Loreto and now here, and you were renting in Las Brisas when I met you. Where to next?

DS. I'm going to rent right downtown in Todos Santos.

MS. That will be different from this house-sit in Gringolandia, just a hop, skip, and a jump from the beach. What do you do for money now? Do you charge for taking people out on tours?

DS. I'm on social security, and I have charged people, because the African trip takes me a year to plan and includes a lot of details. We start in the little town of Maun where I lived and worked, which is right on the edge of the Okavango Delta, the largest inland delta in the world. Next to it is the Moremi Game Reserve. Actually one-third of Botswana is nature reserve. I take people on my favorite camping trip when I lived there: up through the game reserve and into Chobe National Park and then further north to the Zambesi River, ending up at Victoria Falls. Most people I take have never been to Africa and are scared when they hear a lion roar outside their tent. But I like them to think, "If she can do it, then I can do it!"

When I came down in 2015, I thought I wouldn't do any trips with people because they are a lot of work all by myself. But then I met someone, an Italian who loves Baja and who moved to La Paz with his wife a couple years ago. He has a business here, and we have decided to share my ideas and experience with his marketing skills. Our venture will be called Timeless Baja. We will provide tents, vehicles, everything. The trips will be between one to fifteen days. Our website is www.timelessbaja.com. You can drive yourself in a rented four-wheel drive as we lead, or if it's a small group, we go all together in a van. We offer trips to San Ignacio Lagoon to visit the whales and also to the cave paintings. We spend a couple nights in Loreto and do a day-trip into the beautiful Sierra de la Giganta to the old mission there.

The trip to the cave paintings takes about nine days. We stay overnight in a little village in the mountains where there is now a hostel, whereas before we had to camp. We pack up the mules, burros, and gear and meet our guides in the morning. You have to have a guide because the cave paintings are protected, being a UNESCO World Heritage Site, and it is a difficult trip by muleback to get to them. We make camp for two days and hike to the different sites. Then we move camp again and hike to more sites.

It's intimidating to go out in the desert by yourself. If there is a problem, your cell might not work out there. It's a good service that we offer. We have a Facebook page, and I write a blog on the website—not about the tours but about the places. Like, why go to Copper Canyon? What's there? Why do the whales go to the San Ignacio Lagoon? One camper asked me how many times I had been to visit the whales. Sixteen times. The campers said, "And you are still this excited about it?" Well, yeah, I mean the *whales*!

MS. Are there reasons why you like Mexico and Mexican people?

DS. When I was twenty years old, I came with my husband to the Yucatan Peninsula. I had never been out of Seattle, so it was a big eye-opener for me. Number one: getting out of the rain and into the sunshine. And visiting another culture with such a long and different history. The art was fascinating.

MS. What do you think of the Baja culture?

DS. Well, it's mostly a ranch culture. That's why it is considered Mexico's last frontier. But that's what I like about it: the wide-open spaces and places still to explore. I like that the people are so forgiving about us speaking bad Spanish. At least I am trying. My best girlfriend here is Mexican, and I have a good male friend who is Mexican. I make a point to not only associate with Americans or Canadians.

MS. How did you meet them?

DS. My Spanish teacher introduced me to a woman who is widowed and has been in Baja a few years. I am helping her with English, and she is helping me with Spanish. We hit it off as friends. My male friend is a waiter at a restaurant here, and it turns out that he is sixth generation Todosanteños. He took me up to the mountains to show me his family's beautiful ranch, where he and his brother have been building small casitas where people can stay while they hike in the area. Someday it might be offered as one of the tours.

MS. Would you ever consider buying land or a house here?

DS. That was one reason I came—to find out the answer to that question. And the answer is no. People spend so much time and money maintaining their houses here. I don't want to do that. Nobody seems to know how to fix things so that they really *are* fixed. Where I am now, the toilet has been fixed five times in the last two months. If you own and spend time away, you need high security or a house sitter. I don't really want that, and it has taken me a year to decide that. I love it here. I just don't want to buy a house here.

MS. Have you found it difficult or easy to make friends here?

DS. Easy, because the culture allows time to spend with friends. I'm not so tied to my watch. In Santa Fe, I could meet friends for coffee for fifteen minutes. Here we can talk things through. I don't consider myself retired, because I'm in a start-up business. Lots to do on the computer and deciding on the tour curriculum. Should we include this mission? This beach? Things like that.

MS. Have there been challenges here?

DS. The way animals are treated is a constant sorrow to me. It's a bit challenging not to know the language better than I do. When Hurricane Newton came a few weeks back, it was my first experience of being in a hurricane. It's one thing to know about hurricanes; it's another thing to live through one. Just being alone by yourself in a foreign country is challenging. I know a lot of people, so I don't get lonely. Also the gringo community can have differences of opinion, and the atmosphere can get quite emotionally charged. It's best for me not to get involved at all.

MS. Are there any Mexican traits that you like or dislike?

DS. My Spanish teacher is a good bridge between understanding cultural traits as they show up in the language. There is no way to say, "I broke it," in Spanish. Literally you say, "It broke itself." Committing an accident in the old days could reap heavy punishment, so the language supplies a lack of responsibility. That still exists today.

My Italian colleague and I sometimes have communication problems, because his English is not very good and my Italian is nonexistent. At times like that, we use a Spanish phrase: "*La gasolina se acabo.*" The story goes that he went to a three-day music festival here in the Baja, and on the second night, a man on the stage says there will be no more music tonight because "*La gasolina se acabo.*" The gasoline finished itself. End of music festival for that day, because no one filled the generator. It has become the phrase we use when we can't communicate. "*La gasolina se acabo*" to us means "It's screwed; I don't know!"

I am getting more adjusted to this culture. Living in Africa helped me to live here because everything I thought I knew there, I didn't. I had to throw all my many years of training in strategic management in business out the window because it wasn't the way it happens in Africa.

MS. Will you tell me a story about your adventuring life in Baja?

DS. What comes to mind is a trip last year to the cave paintings with ten people. We started out in Loreto, and I told them about the cave paintings being ten thousand years old and so on. Usually the trip is remembered for those incredible paintings. But this trip was different. What was remembered were the people, the Californios, who started the rancho culture in the sierras. Brought from Spain originally to soldier for the Jesuit missionaries, they were handpicked for their wilderness skills some three hundred years ago. They eventually intermarried with the Indians and stayed in the mountains, developing a sustainable culture.

We had a few cowboys who handled and packed the mules. Our main guide, Oscar, no English spoken, was dressed head to foot in home-tanned, homemade chaps, with shoes, saddle, bridles, all made from their ranch tanned hides, Beautiful, and he was so proud of it. The first night a woman in the group (actually my doctor from Santa Fe, New Mexico) took Oscar a plate of food before she ate because she saw how hard he had worked all day. He was stunned that someone should wait on him!

The last night we sat around the campfire, and Oscar told some stories. He said, "You all are different than other people we bring here who are in such a hurry and checking their watches so they can check off where they have been and impatient to get to the next paintings. But you all slowed down and respected us and the animals and this incredible place, where we have never left. Our hearts are the same." People were crying. When we returned to Loreto to spend the last two nights together, we were all different.

We cared for each other. It was so wonderful to see. That is what they took home with them.

Deborah and I spent a few minutes sharing our impressions of a well-made documentary called *Corazon Vaqueros* [Heart of the Cowboys], a movie made by Eve Ewing, Cory McClintock, and Garry McClintock, all veterans of the Baja mountain wilderness terrain. It shows us the daily lives of these *vaqueros* and their families. We experience the peace, humor, and hospitality of a people living as one with their environment and with each other. I was so impressed by the sensitivity and gentleness of the filmmakers' commentary.

Corazon Vaqueros premiered at the Latino Film Festival here in Todos Santos to a full house of appreciative Mexicanos and gringos. What made it special was the presence in the audience of the cowboys, with their stiff white hats, who starred in the movie as they chuckled at themselves on the screen. For some of them, it was their first time out of the mountains, off the rancho, and into another part of the Baja. Afterward they took the stage with the filmmakers, and the audience went wild with applause and a standing ovation. They were being honored for doing what they do, living how they live, and being who they were in some of the most rugged country you could ever imagine. The footage of the mules on the trails heightened my respect for these hardworking, intelligent animals. You can find a shortened version on YouTube, and also the DVD is available on Amazon.

MS. Do you have any advice to the readers of this book?

DS. Don't go exploring the wilderness alone. Be smart; keep thinking. Take precautions. Wear good shoes, and carry a walking stick for balance and snake awareness. Have plenty of water, and drink often.

MS. Have you learned anything about yourself in this move south of the border?

DS. Friends have told me that this is a good place to re-create yourself. If you have a desire to change and decide a focus, you can do it here. I decided to do a spiritual practice with more dedica-tion. I've done parts of it before, but now I do it all every morning. I wake up at five in the morning and actually get up. The natural atmosphere is so quiet, calm, and uncomplicated at that hour. For an hour, I meditate, write affirmations, and exercise. The exercise is really important. It's a powerful practice, because I can actually make progress in my commitment to feel good.

MS. Thanks for your time, and good luck on your endeavor to share this incredible place with the people who come here and also us residents, who desire to see more. You offer knowledge and experience and a cool head. Your love of place is palpable.

CHAPTER 20

GILLIAN HERBERT

I arrived at Gillian's small rental in colonia Las Brisas on a hot afternoon in July. She suggested the time and place because she had air conditioning in the bedroom. Where else was there to be at four in the afternoon in July? In front of a fan, at least. I noticed that the bougainvillea in front of the bay window close to the street had grown up enough to do what she wanted it to do: be a dust trap from the road traffic and create shade from the afternoon sun. Life had to be more comfortable for her now. The last time I saw her, she had a terrible cough and sore throat from the dust blowing on the almost continuous ocean breeze, after all *Las Brisas*" means "the breezes." It was a very busy street, and near the bottom of the hill was the *bomberos*, which is Spanish for pumpers or, in this case, fireman. Thanks to gringo-inspired benefits, it was outfitted with pumper trucks and ambulances.

Here, too, was a canine greeting: Lucy, a five-year-old Rottweiler, who was acting like I was her best friend finally coming for a visit. Gillian had always kept a big guard dog and trained them all well. She advised me to do likewise, but the German-shepherd rescue dog I brought home turned out to be very aggressive although playful. I kept apologizing to my older dog for having brought her home. But that's another story.

Gillian's rental cost her three thousand pesos a month and had everything a house should have, including a nice, private, breeze-blocked porch, perfect for leaving Lucy on when Gillian went out. We settled into the bedroom with some icy drinks and began to talk. Gillian is in comfortable clothes and nestles into the bed because she has been spending lots of time there recovering from hip surgery. She alternates between bright and cheery and lined and frowning as she tells me her life story.

Gillian Herbert (GH). I am seventy-seven and a half and first came to Mexico in 1963, when I was twenty-five. I had been working for Bahama Airlines for two years and was shipping out to the Orient to work in a hotel but decided to go home to Vancouver, British Columbia, Canada, first. After two weeks at home, I was so bored out of my tree that I decided to swap my ticket for the Orient to Mexico City for three weeks and ended up staying three years!

Friends there showed me around, and I loved the city in those days. I went to the theater, listened to the mariachis every night, and went to the discos. I was very happy in Mexico City. They started building hotels, and while walking to work, I was a target for the workers, who threw bits of concrete at me to get my attention. I am blond and blue eyed and stuck out like a sore thumb.

My friend suggested that I go to Acapulco because I would be just one more *tourista*. I went and landed a job there as executive secretary to the manager of a new hotel. I was quite fluent in Spanish because I had been living with a Mexican family in Mexico City for three years and working for a Mexican company that hired me because of my English. They had just acquired an American partner and had no one who knew English. My advice to younger people is to learn another language. Don't put that aside as not a priority, because being bilingual, you can work anywhere in the world, as I did.

I loved Acapulco and was soon stolen away to work at the Hyatt Regency that was just opening. I met lots of movie stars there. Then the Hilton asked if I would go to Okinawa, Japan, to help open their hotel there. Because I have an adventurous spirit, I thought it was a great opportunity to get to the Orient. What a terrible mistake! When I look back, it was probably the worst mistake I have ever made.

It was a comedown to go from the PR director of the Hyatt Regency in Acapulco to a tiny island where there were only air-force people. There was no place to eat but tiny stands selling dried cockroaches! Oh! There was one hotel, a couple of restaurants, and you couldn't go on the base where they had American-style food. There were one hundred fifty thousand American servicemen and their families on the island. I was to be a liaison between the military and the hotel to know when VIPs were coming, about troop movements, and so. My boss called me Mata Hari. Whenever I went to the base, they would shuttle me into the generals' quarters because there were no other Western civilian women, and they entertained me for hours.

MS. Was there something in your past or your personality that set you up for travel to foreign lands?

GH. My parents emigrated to Canada from England when I was sixteen. I had been to college and had worked, so I was a bit of a free agent on the ship and on the train. I was not afraid to talk to strangers. I think it endowed me with the confidence that it takes to travel. I was the perfect age to develop it, and I never had the negative energy young people can have. I think it was because I grew up in England during World War II and my parents never showed fear or negativity. That gave me confidence.

MS. So did you stay in Japan long?

GH. No. During a typhoon, I got hepatitis A, and I was in hospital in Hong Kong for a month. They recommended six months of complete rest, so I went back to my parent's house in Vancouver.

Upon my recovery, the Mexican National Tourist Council opened an office in Vancouver, and they hired me as executive secretary to the boss because I was bilingual and already had quite a lot of Mexican experience in Mexico City and Acapulco. I set up promotional events, found and hired mariachi bands, and was sort of a sales director. I did that for two years.

In 1972, an old friend walked into the office and said he was going to start doing tours to Cabo San Lucas. I asked, "Where's that?" He asked, "What are you doing?" I replied, "Trying to get back to Mexico. I don't really like living in Vancouver." He said, "You have a job then in Cabo San Lucas." So in 1973, the first tour groups came to Cabo. I drove an old van with two friends from San Francisco and worked with the tour company for two years.

MS. Wow! What was Cabo like back then?

GH. Tiny and lovely! [*She laughed a big, hearty laugh at the memory.*] There was one paved road into the middle of town, and then it stopped. All the other roads were dirt. No marina. One dingy dock, only a few marlin fishing boats. No shipping.

MS. Well, what did you think of your tourist job then?

GH. I thought it would attract people who wanted to see and be in a small Mexican town off the beaten path. I set up little tours to the goat farm and to the mission school to meet the Mexican kids, and the kids could practice their English. I taught English at the school when I wasn't doing anything else.

MS. Where did the tourists stay?

GH. There were three hotels: El Mar de Cortez, which is still there, with twenty rooms, the Finestra with twelve rooms, and the Hacienda Hotel with twenty rooms. Of course it was only for the winter season, so I traveled around Mexico with a boyfriend the rest of the year. Eventually I became assistant to the manager of the Hyatt in Cabo for three years. The owners were Mexican, and many rich and VIP Mexicans came to Cabo.

I realized that there was no travel agency in Cabo, so I started one with some settlement money from a union settlement I got when I was fired from the Cabo Bello, which came under new management by a German guy who wanted my job for his wife. In Mexico, you cannot fire someone.

Your readers should understand that Mexico is not a Western culture from the very base up. It has laws that are incomprehensible to foreigners. It is good to try to understand what you are getting into when you do something down here. It is a very classist and racist culture. Not only the color of your skin but also Indian features will draw you down. Mexicans are afraid of foreigners and are hesitant to negate your needs, so they never say no. Because if they did so in the old days, something negative would happen to them.

MS. Are you a Mexican citizen?

GH. No. In the old days, there was no emigration and no defining status. I don't care to vote. I am a world citizen. I already have Canadian and English passports, so I don't need another one.

MS. Have you ever owned land here?

GH. Yes. I bought a lot on the hill they call the Pedrigal in Cabo San Lucas. I built the second house on the hill and later sold it, because there was a renter who wouldn't pay. Here the renter has all the rights. If you rent, be sure to have a proper contract drawn up...something in print.

MS. So how did the tourist trade go?

GH. I invented lots of tours. I hired *pongas* [*small boats used by fisherman and as water taxis to off road places on the shoreline*] to take people out. The first time I had a group of thirty tourists scheduled to go out at eight in the morning, there had been a big fiesta for St. Luke, the patron saint of Cabo San Lucas, the night before. One *ponga* driver showed up drunk. I quickly hired all the marlin boats, and the tourists went out. But it cost me everything I might have earned. I talked to the port authority about it, and I used the street slang for drunk, which is *"pedo,"* meaning fart. I was very unpopular after that. It was the wrong thing to say.

MS. Live and learn, I guess. I know you had a Mexican husband at one point. When was that?

GH. It was when he and I worked at the Hyatt Regency. He was kind and energetic and entrepreneurial. He had a good head for business, and for five or six years. we did the travel agency together. When we started making money, he started drinking. A tour group came from England, so I decided to separate from the husband and Mexico and go back to England.

MS. I see that you are not afraid to move on when things get uncomfortable or a better opportunity arises. You are entrepreneurial, confident, and competent.

GH. And I'm a good salesman! [*She smiled and nodded her head.*] Not everyone is. But I'm not afraid to talk to strangers and hear their situations, and maybe I can help them out.

MS. So how long were you in Europe?

GH. For four years, I was a tour guide in Spain, near Barcelona. Spain is the most fun country for a tour guide. There were lots of us, and we had fun and made money! When I got back to Cabo, I dealt with the renter in my house, so after a lawsuit, I sold cheap and was offered a position in Mulege, up the peninsula on the Sea of Cortez side. It was a run-down hotel, which needed fixing and basically everything. There was not much money to work with, but I traded for labor, like getting some signs painted and put out on the highway.

Next I noticed some strangers in town, and upon talking with them, I learned that they were chefs from Paris on vacation and looking for a place to stay. I invited them to stay at the hotel for free if they would cook in the kitchen. They asked, "What's for dinner?" I had just bought lobster, so we all happily jaunted over to the hotel. They stayed a month and rearranged the kitchen, set it up to function, and I soon had a clientele of people coming to the restaurant. The next opportunity happened by way of an English physicist, who stayed for free in trade for plumbing the next ten rooms. It all worked out fine until I was visited by emigration and they saw I didn't have the papers to work in Mexico.

On the road again, this time in an old van, I ended up in La Paz, where I managed an apartment complex. Once again I would talk to people walking on the *malecon* and ask them where they were staying. I filled the place up. I then went back to Canada to be with my mother and father while they aged. Being a loyal daughter and a dedicated caregiver, I stayed for twelve years. I was a little depressed but was happy also.

After their deaths, I sold the house, paid the debts, and bought a motor home, which I drove down to Baja every winter and back to Canada every spring. I had a reputation for knowing the Baja and was asked to be a guide for a film crew going there. From that experience, I created a video of driving the Baja, and for six years, I taught a one-week seminar in Canada at Okanagan College for free, sharing my love and knowledge of the peninsula. The guy who bought my first copy drove down here four years ago and lived in paradise until two months ago when he died here at age eighty-four.

MS. I got to know him. He certainly enjoyed his last years here. How did you come to Todos Santos?

GH. At one point I had a wonderful house-sitting job at Punta Chivato, about forty miles north of Mulege. It was very beautiful, right on the Sea of Cortez, on a beautiful bay called Sta. Inez, with other single homes owned by foreigners. The beach was littered with shells for collecting. In spite of its beauty, there was no town center, so all socialization happened by invitation. I got caught in the exclusion trap of a single woman. The houses had been built in neighborhoods, and these promoted cliques of location with people rarely leaving their private beachfronts and adjacent friends.

One lonely Christmas day when I had nowhere to go, my Mexican helper asked me to come to her house for the celebration. Good Mexican people, coming from the heart, and I'm sure my ability to speak Spanish opened many doors.

A friend who had rented from me in La Paz had relocated in Todos Santos and encouraged me to check it out, as there were lots of single, strong women there and a bit of culture, too. I taught Spanish in Punta Chivato and other places I have lived, and I find it is a great way to get to know people. I did the same in Todos Santos. The classes were offered for free, and it is a good way to meet the community by giving. Sometimes I would have twenty to thirty people in the classes, but now that I charge fifty pesos, I have five.

Gillian let out a big, loud laugh here as she laughed at the inevitable twists of life, which she was old enough to have witnessed in her near seventy-eight years.

GH. It is important to know the language, enough to communicate to a doctor. Many doctors and health-care providers have attitudes about gringos coming and using their welfare insurance, Seguro Popular. They won't speak to the patient in English, even if the doctor is quite fluent in English. You need a Spanish-speaking advocate in a hospital here.

Right now in my life, I am so disillusioned with Mexico. I'm in a very bad, sad place with Mexico, because it has changed so much in the fifty years I've been coming here. I am seriously thinking of leaving.

MS. Where would you go? What is the difference you see?

GH. I might go to Cuba or Spain or Canada, anywhere. It's not just Mexico; it's what change has brought to the whole world in the last fifty years. It's become a marketplace; it's all about the bottom line, getting as much as you can for as little effort as you need to make. The world has changed.

In Mexico, the workers hear, "I would have paid four times that in the States!" and so they look at the gringos now as a money supply: "How much money can I get off of you?" Before, they were genuinely warm and interested that you had come to Mexico. I feel like I am racially profiled every time I go to buy something. Of course poor Mexicans have always been helpful if you break down on the highway. Poor people the world over know that helping each other out is a necessary survival aid. They are the real Mexicans. The professionals and shop owners keep raising their prices.

I don't want to get into a situation here at my age where I couldn't speak or advocate for myself. I think I need to go where I can get medical attention if I need it. England or Canada, because I have passports for those countries. Speaking of Cuba, they have lovely people who are not spoiled yet. They have free health care and good doctors. Canada has supported and traded with Cuba through the US embargo for many years. They do like Canadians for aiding them when they were starving. I have been there but haven't checked it out online lately.

I couldn't take an English winter, but traveling in the European Union is cheap. I can go to southern France or Spain or Crete or Greece for the winter and still get my pension from the United Kingdom. That appeals to me. Or go to Majorca, off the African coast, where the winters are warm.

MS. At your age, do you think you have the energy to make a move like that, even seasonally?

GH. I do have to think of that, and I have a very small income. So I have to go somewhere where it is inexpensive to live, like here. I am just keeping my head above water here. My income from Canada just pays the rent on the house. Period. So without the Spanish students, neither my dog nor I would eat, nor would I be able to run my car.

Another thing that makes me sad is that there is no music to my liking here. It's all American music, cowboy, country and western, rock 'n' roll. We have no beautiful Mexican music here. Where are the mariachi players tonight, tomorrow night? We have none.

Baja is a vacuum of culture. It was isolated for so many years, peopled by fisherman, Indians, and missionaries who brought the ranchero culture from Spain. The culture of the mainland never came here. As much as it is beautiful here and we love it, it is turning into something different...into California South, honey. I don't want to live in the American culture; it is not my culture. There are too many gringos here, and more and more are coming every single day. If I lived in Canada, maybe I would try subleasing this house and come back in the winter.

MS. Have you thought of the mountain climate of the mainland Mexico, said to be perpetual spring? Or the harp music in Veracruz? Lovely. Have you considered that?

GH. I have lived many places, and there was always plenty to do. But here, right now, I am bored to death! I watch Mexican TV and listened the other day to lovely bolero music and then the African-influenced music. It was so beautiful, I burst out crying. Where do you go to hear music? The bars are playing American music.

Later, after the day of this interview, I made sure to invite Gillian to the Hotel California on Sunday to hear Antonio play guitar and sing traditional songs. Gillian knew many of the songs and sang along with Antonio, who sang in harmony with a pleasant smile on his face. I picked her up several Sundays in a row just to see her face light up with pleasure.

Gillian was missing the undeniable magic of mainland Mexico—and perhaps her youth—and traveling and working at her own discretion and will. No matter where you are living, aging probably brings up these feelings, like surviving heat, hurricanes, isolation; fearing inevitable death; and being with or without proper medical assistance.

We exited the cool bedroom and emerged into the heat of the kitchen counter and had a delicious meal prepared by Gillian. She loved to entertain and cook for others. I guess we will all face some of these same questions as we live here. I have noticed that there seems to be a time limit on the dream of moving here. Between twelve and sixteen years, people start wanting something a little easier, like speaking their first language to a clerk or a doctor.

We love the tropical palms that don't grow in Wisconsin, but we don't love the aftereffects of a hurricane. We love our gringo friends here, and we are a creative bunch, inventing ways to help out and ways to entertain ourselves. We love our Mexican friends here who have shared their families, skills, and traditions with us foreigners. Many people are hermits in their fenced paradises and enjoy the freedom of anonymity and the lack of pressure to socialize. And we are always changing in our own lives, our needs, and our desires, according to our ages and histories and futures. Good luck, Gillian!

After I turned off the recorder, Gillian told a story of her mystical initiation into her Mexican sojourn, which had lasted fifty years. When she first arrived in Mexico City at age twenty-five with the desire to learn Spanish, she lived in an apartment above a travel agency. They would arrange tours for students around the city and beyond. One day they asked her if she wanted to go with some students to visit a huge statue that had just been discovered and was being unearthed near Teotihuacan, the city of pyramids north of the city.

Of course she went. The statue was of the rain god Tlaloc and was nestled in the earth of a field. Only his nose had been visible for centuries, and for years, the locals had been chipping away at the granite rock because it was the only such rock around. Gillian said that the nose alone was as big as the bedroom we were sitting in. At this time the statue had been dug out but still lay in its resting place. The students climbed onto the face and sat on the nose of the rain god.

Along came a Mexicano with a bucket of *pulque,* an agave liquor with a long history in the country. He asked if they wanted some. "Oh, yes!" the students replied. They sipped the *pulque* there on the nose, no doubt altering their consciousness a bit.

At this point, Gillian believed, the spirit of Mexico grabbed at her heart and called her name to live and love and adventure in Mexico. She said that they eventually moved the massive statue to the anthropological museum in the city and left it on the steps outside because it was too big to get in the door. When the statue was in place, she said, it poured rain for a week. Perhaps the rain god, Tlaloc, was honored and happy to be freed of his grave and in public admiration once again.

AFTER THOUGHTS

What, you might ask me, do these 20 women have in common besides their choice to live south of the border? They all have different histories and talents brought to this present moment, and different objectives in their everyday decisions on how to spend their time now. To find a common thread to string these beautiful pearls-of-girls on is a challenge, but a few commonalities stand out.

One intangible is their overall positive outlook. They tend to accept the moment, be it strange, foreign, or frightening. They don't frighten easily or give up on a dream. Were they always like this, or is love of this place and life-style enough for them to relax around the changes that life still presents? They want to be here, so they remain strong in their personal power and commitment to self-determination. Retirement brings with it pleasing yourself, such as designing your new home as an expression of your previous wisdom acquired and future ambitions. Often to live alone is to fill time at a leisurely pace. "I don't do 'hurry' anymore" and "I only do what I like," are 2 phrases you hear often. This slows the flow and reduces anxiety. These women aren't grumpy!

All of them talk of the challenges that they face on a daily basis and then feel strong in themselves because they stepped up and faced them. Some solutions require adopting new skills and others require letting go of old habits of reactivity. Mexican culture tends to be more laid back than American culture, so there is less stress about questions of what to do or how to handle a situation. It feels less aggressive here. Time isn't pressing at your back. They all acknowledge the lessons they have learned here and are happy to pass them on. Aging issues come up at this time of life anywhere we live. In Mexico, there can be different solutions, or no solutions. You're on your own, backed up by the modern world of communication and air travel.

I was curious to know how dependent the ex-pat community is on the internet and computers in general. I would say: quite a lot. It is the connection to family and friends left behind and the greater world outside this skinny frontier peninsula. One of the women never had a computer and just recently got a device. For others reception goes on and off and thus is not a constant to rely on. Conclusion: We would all be forlorn if we couldn't be entertained and informed in our cloistered paradise away from the modern world civilization.

When I first started living here I could see that a large percentage of ex-pats were not your typical Americans. They were adventurers, outdoor people, counterculture drop outs, risk takers, low budget survivors, optimists, freedom seekers grateful to be out of restrictive cultural dictates and definitions. When Anita Trammell said "You have to be a bubble off to live here," I laughed because I have witnessed the bubble-off people. It is a carpenter's term describing the bubble in the glass tube of a carpenter's level. When the bubble's in the center, the 2x4 is vertical or the table top is straight on the horizontal. To be a "bubble off" means you're not straight!

It is nice to start again when the one road to town starts feeling like a rut... a long drawn out grave...going nowhere really slowly. To have new challenges is stimulating. I often tell my friends that moving here in my late 50's was the best thing I could have done...

everything was new and it stimulated my attention and my seeking out new information. Among these women are those applying old skills to new situations and entrepreneurs feeling their way into new income streams. I guess it really is like life anywhere, but you put it in a foreign country, Mexico in particular, and you have a new flavor, vibrant colors, Latin tempos and you're surrounded by people who smile easily, have family relations in the area and simple diets. So along with life and all its trials, you also have fun! Tequila helps!

One theme that runs thru some, not all, of these interviews is money. Every modern person works for money in some capacity. By asking each one how much she lives on a month, I hope to give the curious reader a gage for decision making. America is getting more and more expensive to live in. Less living expenses is better for the fixed income crowd, so I hope the fullness of these women's lives gives the reader an idea of how life can happen on a slender budget.

Strangely, spirituality goes along with money-talk. Faith being the issue, and the perspective of most of your Mexican neighbors and workers who live on so little money and are so happy. Quite a few of the interviewees have a strong sense of the divine guidance that advises them on issues grand and small. For them the most important issue is to be true to themselves and their guidance. They recall being guided here to live. There is a strong spirit of nature in the desert because there is so much more land than man-made structures. We cannot discount the pull of spirit-of-place when Anita Harris says, "I'm becoming a bit of a nature freak!" From an office worker in London to nature freak, Anita acknowledges the profound change for the better that her abrupt move made in her life.

Lastly, I asked each participant her impressions of Mexican culture and Mexicans. Even though they have similar complaints and dissatisfactions, they are temperate with their criticism because they know they are guests in a foreign country. American visitors (tourists and friends) tend to see this place thru the eyes of middle-class Americans. How else could they see it? When you live here for a while, you acknowledge that this is *not* America and it silences you into respectful observation. I spent some time reading books from the library on Mexican history and how it relates to modern-day practices and beliefs. There are reasons for never telling a gringo "no," even if it is a correct answer. I watched a Mexican friend who is a para-legal help people through the legal maze of bureaucracy in the offices in La Paz. He was so polite, never ruffling a feather, gracefully and smoothly achieving a complicated goal. But, of course, Spanish has polite verb endings and phrases that helped him. The demeanor of his culture smoothed the way, *muy amable.*

By reading this book I hope you find inspiration for your future if you are desiring change, or at least enjoy the tales of modern women navigating the aging process through changing their locations, neighbors, language, diets, friends...a whole new slice of life!